PRAISE FOR
The Art of Being Whole

Copploe fills his pages with delightful anecdotes that inspire the reader to think beyond our ritualistic journey, and to explore our sense of self and higher purpose. The poetic divisions between chapters are delightful and thought provoking. **-Sue Beller, Author Recipe for Peace Now**

***

The Art of Being Whole is an insightful journey of the mind as we minimize our ego and supplement humility and kindness to achieve something greater and more purposeful. The poetry between chapters was a fresh inhalation. I deeply understood the author's journey, and his ability to cocoon and morph into a beautiful butterfly time and again. *-Mary Eversole, Executive Director, Vermont Insurance Agents Association*

What a big journey this man had, and his childhood broke my heart, but to see him come full circle is completely joyful. We all have the chance and ability to change and move forward to become our greatest potential. This book inspired me to be greater, better, kinder, and more loving. We need more books like this in the world during a time of upheaval and chaos. Bravo. *-Kristy Watson, Chief Marketing Office, Erno Laszlo Skin Care*

***

The Art of Being Whole defines our uniqueness and it reaffirms that we are all beautiful no matter what journey we are on, and no matter what body shell we have borrowed to live a spiritual existence. The stories were extremely entertaining, and I loved the spiritual messages weaved throughout, including the poetry.
-Marlene Cuesta, CEO MC Licensing (Premium Entertainment Brands)

THE ART
OF BEING
WHOLE

A personal account of grit, love, and fearless living

GREGORY COPPLOE

GREGORY COPPLOE

Published by KHARIS PUBLISHING, imprint of
KHARIS MEDIA LLC.

Copyright © 2019 Gregory Copploe

ISBN-13: 978-1-946277-40-4
ISBN-10: 1-946277-40-1

Library of Congress Control Number: 2019948226

All KHARIS PUBLISHING products are available at
special quantity discounts for bulk purchase for sales
promotions, premiums, fund-raising, and educational
needs. For details, contact:

Kharis Media LLC
Tel: 1-479-599-8657
support@kharispublishing.com
www.kharispublishing.com

TABLE OF CONTENTS

Anne:
Hope you enjoy the book.
Thanks for being such a
beautiful light for our
team.

Love + Light

Greg Coombe

X

INTRODUCTION

This book is autobiographical and at the same time a reflection of my conscious mind as I traverse through a multitude of experiences and grow to realize certain truths and beliefs that end up shaping my existence.

I believe we are all a bit broken, and there is so much beauty in that brokenness. As a society we are all so quick to judge, and so critical of ourselves, that we fail to embrace our uniqueness as something of value. We are beautiful, and it is this uniqueness that makes us even more so. I didn't understand many of these truths, as I embarked on my life journey, but I knew someday wisdom would inhabit my soul. I understood that there was something greater, and I understood that it had power and deeper meaning.

There was a connection inside me that wanted to connect to something bigger than myself, and thus my spiritual journey began. I will begin and end some sections with poems that I have integrated into the book. Poetry and I have a deep connection, and we seem to understand each other very well. When I began this adventure, I desired to write a book of poetry, and then realized through my poetry, that I had a story to tell, and I could weave both into a delicious meal that we could all digest together without getting a charge of indigestion or acid reflux.

I believe we all have a story to tell, and each one of us is equally important as we search for our sense of purpose and alignment on Planet Earth. Occasionally we lose our way. We pray that we find a semblance of purpose, that provides some joy and happiness, as we persevere learning more about ourselves and our uniqueness. We are all one species, and this joyful statement connects each and every one of us together through spirit, even though our packaging may come in a variety of colors, shapes and sizes. We must understand our connectedness in order to respect our uniqueness. This way, we can thrive in a harmonious state of being.

My journey will encompass love, heartbreak, and everything in between. I will search and discover what love and light truly mean, as the rock I am encased in is shattered, to reveal the diamond beneath.

Being broken is a gift that allows us to reach the bottom of the abyss and slowly ascend upward toward the light without ego; we embrace love, humility and purpose. The metaphor of the shattered encasement, in fact, reveals our truth, our core essence of being. I think we can all understand why being a bit broken can be so utterly beautiful.

"We are not human beings having a spiritual experience. We are spiritual beings having a human experience." — *Father Pierre Teilhard de Chardin*

On that note, let the journey begin. I dedicate this book to my mother, Karole Ann Sieroty, and my father, Glenn Anthony Copploe. They shaped my beginnings; I wouldn't be the same without them, nor would my journey. My final dedication goes to Noha Omar and Javier Tordable, who have stood by my side, celebrating life and lifting me up when I had no wings to fly, and I consider them my family.

CHAPTER 1

Home

*I cannot see the steps I take to move forward
thus
Yet I take them with a fervor and delicious stride
Never knowing where my feet will land
But certain each step is purposeful and
enlightened
As I begin my journey each day upward toward
the light*

I have learned through listening to the stories of others, that many, if not all of us, come from broken childhoods. Mine was the same. I won't spend too much time with my childhood, as I think it would be too painful for the reader, and for myself, so we will highlight certain areas that helped propel me on my journey toward enlightenment.

It was a fresh winter day in Northern California. The small puddles were frozen on the ground, and it always amazed me when this happened. I thought the puddles and thin layer of ice were so perplexing and beautiful as I would walk home from elementary school. I'd find a stick along the path and pretend it was my magic stick, that would protect me from the evil in the world. The stick would skip each square in the pavement, and slip into the groove of each one, with a small thud, as it bounced back and repeated itself through each broken space of the sidewalk.

I was approximately eight years old, heading home from another successful day at school, where I excelled and wowed my peers with my bit of knowledge and childlike expertise, or as much expertise as a child could contain at the undeveloped year of eight. In short, I would fill out the answer sheet for the teacher in red pen, while the rest of the students took their tests, and was touted as a gifted student by many of the faculty.

I wouldn't find out until much later that I really didn't know much at all, but nonetheless I was full of myself and confident that I would succeed and escape my current plight, which was, for the most part, sad and abusive. I turned the corner on Bluegrass Lane, a small street in San Jose, California, where my mom and stepfather bought a small townhome. They insisted it was their small mansion in the sky, where they could live out their dreams.

There was a hint of garlic in the air that day; a nearby garlic factory continued churning out millions of peeled cloves, which would be flown out daily, to destinations across the U.S. As I turned the corner and inched closer to the house, my heart began to race. It was a normal Pavlovian fear, that slowly crept in, as I turned that corner and stood there gazing at my home. I had childhood anxiety. It would escalate as I dropped my left hand into my pants pocket, to dig for the keys that would open the unpredictable door, exposing a new adventure that usually went awry.

I gently lifted my key, softly sliding it into the keyhole and cautiously opened the door. My mom was strewn out in her bathrobe, napping in what looked like a peaceful slumber. But looks can be deceiving. There was nothing peaceful about my mother, nor her ability to relax and enjoy a peaceful state of existence. Waking my mom up would cost me dearly, so I did my best to tiptoe around. I began to ascend the small carpeted staircase toward my room, much like a cat that makes little to no sound, as it slinks its paws on the fluffy carpeted surface.

Sadly, it was too late. My mom pounced awake, as one of the stairs creaked with instability and broke her peaceful slumber. She intuitively felt my presence, and she certainly had a psychic way about her that always perplexed me. Her voice sounded shrill as she would hiss in pain, recovering from back surgery at the time, and quite addicted to a variety of opiates. She was disconnected at best and according to therapists, that I had visited upon my mother's request, I was told she had a personality disorder; my stepfather and I would later discover it was acute schizophrenia.

The year was 1972, and people weren't so openly diagnosed with disorders and put on medications like they are now. Many turned a blind eye to mental disorders, and I took the brunt of their lack of diligence. I stood halfway up the stairs facing my mother, who was now fully awake, and she stood at the bottom of the stairs and told me to come down. She had a gift for me. Her voice was kind and loving, which was unusual at the time, so I went with the current mood and hoped for the best.

She had kind moments where she would express love but they were fleeting and quite momentary. She went upstairs and into her room, where she vanished for about two minutes and then reappeared at the top of the staircase. She stood there, staring at me with a vacuous look on her face. The blank stare sent chills up my spine, my arm hairs stood straight up toward the ceiling, as if they were plants garnering photosynthesis from the sun. There was no reasoning with her, so one just tried to go with the flow and hope that it didn't turn too scary.

I knew something was very wrong and I knew my mother had some serious illness. I think that's what saved me from taking anything too seriously, although, I truly did feel like I was in danger all the time. She came downstairs, the jugular vein in her neck beginning to protrude on both the left and right, as her voice escalated. She was upset that I was standing at the bottom of the stairs, with no purpose other than to wait for her with a supposed gift, that she promised she would bestow upon me. Her approach was swift as her bottom teeth protruded, touching the soft part of her upper lip, and her left hand swung around to crack me across the face. There was no reasoning behind it other than I was annoying her simply by being present in the room.

These little games ensued daily and snowballed right into dinnertime. Dinnertime was a strange debacle, right out of some archaic horror show, as I was told to shower, dress up, and sit up straight in my chair while the food was being served. I wasn't allowed to reach toward the table, and my mother had a saying, "Keep your elbows off the table; this isn't a horses' stable."

If food were to land on my clothing and not in my mouth, I would be excused from the table without dinner and go hungry until the next morning. It was a sordid torture and, eventually I learned with precision to land every piece, including a saucy one, into my mouth without spilling a drop. Not your typical childhood, but then again, I am not sure anyone had a normal one in the seventies. I flowed through the tests and obstacles as best I could or as anyone could, as a small child.

The scenarios would change, but the story played the same, again and again, as the mental disorder worsened over time. Often I would be disturbed at 3:00 a.m. and told to clean the bathtub because there was some dirt around the rim or something distasteful sitting near the metal drain. It's no wonder I developed a sleeping disorder. I felt unsafe as a child, and this progressed into my adult life. I truly felt sorry for my mother, and there was a part of me that understood that she was trapped in a body shell that didn't function well, and she wanted out. I felt helpless as she flipped from one character to the next. It was clear that my sordid torture was an internal lashing from her own insanity.

No one escaped the torture and, at times, I felt my stepfather received a bludgeoning so much worse than mine. His hair was pulled, while being knocked about, until falling from his chair and landing on the thick shag carpet below. He was a gentleman and would never hit a woman, so he basically sat there and absorbed her wrath as she shredded any pride and integrity he had left. He did try and leave her several times, but she was quite manipulative, and her crying outbursts always lured him back. She ran the show, and it was one of the most unique sideshows we had ever seen. She battered us for hours both mentally and physically until she collapsed with exhaustion.

If any of you have seen the movie *Mommy Dearest,* I would say that was pretty much my homelife scenario, and Mary Tyler Moore in *Ordinary People* did a great job of portraying my mother. Both movies encapsulated a great summation of my homelife. My mother was an extravagant individual, came from a rich family of furriers, yet she never seemed to have enough money of her own. She lived in her own frail bubble, believing she was some famous movie actress, that the world owed her some kind of elaborate gift, just because she was on the planet, bestowing her presence for all to see. It was quite delusional, but acute mental illness can create a vortex in the cerebral cortex of one's mind. That delusion can appear quite real.

I didn't understand the nuances completely, but I loved my mother. I forgave her endlessly, simply craving one small moment in time, where we could connect and share a brief interlude of love. It would be this connected moment that would carry me through the darkness, as I would forgive her repeatedly, and yearn for just one more moment where we would interact as a normal mother and son.

Thankfully I knew my homelife wasn't normal, and I knew the world was vast, so I stayed focused in school, knowing that college was my golden ticket. I worked hard and moved forward with an intense passion. I would ensure I got out of this debilitating situation and onward to some normalcy of life.

Others somehow knew and understood my homelife situation. They offered me a place to stay or a shoulder to cry on, as I would arrive to school with bruises or marks on my face that I didn't have the day prior. I would make up stories, telling everyone I bumped my head on a door, but they were a bit smarter than I was, and knew about my abusive homelife. When I would visit friends' homes, it became clearer that my situation was definitely "abbey normal" (*Young Frankenstein* reference), yet I somehow understood that it was temporary, and my new life was already transporting itself into view. I just needed to believe that I could have a more fulfilling existence, and with that simple thought, it shaped itself to become just that: A world so real, designed by my own thoughts and purified by my imagination.

There is no sense torturing myself or the reader further with mangling stories of my childhood, but I will tell you that I learned, later, that my past didn't have to define me. And it wasn't an excuse for why I didn't achieve or excel at something. It was simply a learning experience, that would help me understand something much greater, as I searched for my higher purpose.

By sixteen years old I realized that it was time to leave my current dysfunctional situation and I had lots of offers of places to stay, so I could continue my education and apply for my colleges of choice. I knew I couldn't stay until I was eighteen, as each day was completely unbearable, and was starting to get in the way of my studies and goals. The vice principal of my high school used to be a nun, and she invited me to stay with her. We had an excellent connection, and she understood me well. I was also a member of the speech and debate team in high school. My speech coach also offered to have me stay with her. I excelled at speech and debate and won several awards in high school. It was very clear what I needed to do. If I excelled at the speech and debate competition, then I would stay longer at the tournament. If I made it to the finals, I stayed even longer.

The team traveled to each tournament, so making it to finals was key to give me a break from my homelife, for a weekend or two. I made sure I made it to the finals round, every time I performed. I would learn later in life that I was actually good at performing, but I didn't understand this skillset and how it would benefit me in the future. For now it was just a survival technique I excelled in, in order to find some peace and sanity away from home.

I was also working at a pizza place and an auto stereo store, and had offers, from the owners, to come stay with them as well. It seemed the world wanted to rescue me from my plight, and I was so thankful and grateful that I had so many offers. I was involved in theater, the National Honor Society, swim team, and diving team, and I had offers from so many gracious people. The world was out to save me, but who would save me from myself?

I ended up staying with a friend of mine who ran the high school newspaper, and it seemed like a good fit at the time. Rather than jump into a scenario with someone I didn't really know, I felt more comfortable staying with someone my own age and sharing his family. Little did I know that this journey would reveal dark little secrets that would inevitably rip his family apart, and I would be the catalyst of it all, or at least the one to assist in exposing the sinister truth.

I had only been there a few days, was getting ready for bed one evening, stripped down to my underwear and preparing for a little workout before sinking into my bedsheets. As I was working out, I heard a knock on my door, and it was my friend's father. He began conversing with me. He left a check on the bedroom bureau for forty dollars and told me that I was a good boy. I thought it was odd, but I really needed the money for college, so I thanked him and continued doing my sit-ups, not thinking much of it at the time.

Then he lurched in the doorway, staring at me, his lower lip began to quiver. He asked me softly if I could lower my underwear. I politely declined and sat there stunned as the door closed and he departed. I now had a check on my bureau, evidence of his visit, and I needed to speak with my friend in the morning.

It was a long night with little-to-no sleep and morning couldn't arrive fast enough. Prior to departing for school, I grabbed my friend and explained the strange visit from his father. I presented him with the mysterious forty-dollar check. Teary eyed and distraught, he explained to me that he was molested by his father, as a child, but never told his mother.

It was a dark, scary secret that he had kept

all these years, scared to come forward and destroy the façade of marriage that his mother so cherished for decades. The father felt the shift in energy inside the house, after he left that dirty check on my bureau the evening prior, declining his offer to expose my nude self while he could watch and enjoy. He began verbally attacking me the day after, calling me the son of Satan, and ordered me to leave the house immediately. After a stringent assault of verbal abuse, my friend felt compelled to tell his mother the truth. That was my last day at his house and the last day of their marriage.

I believe the darkness of his secret festered for quite some time as he eventually lost his mind. He later held up a local Burger King with a shotgun and become incarcerated after that. I don't believe he hurt anyone except himself. Such a sad story and such a tormented soul who kept too much inside, for too many years.

Homeward bound I was, back into the darkness and dysfunction, unable to escape to some brighter plateau, where I could relax and just take a breath for a moment. I was beginning to believe that we simply all lived in Hell, and there was no happy place, although I had seen some glimpses of love and happiness at other households.

I assumed they were facades where two people committed their lives together, through compromise and dark secrets, that were hidden from view. That they went on hoping that the secrets were never exposed, so they could live their lies together and formulate what they called "true love."

I was home for about two miserable days before I packed another suitcase; I was on-board to try another adventure. My stepfather held the door, as he told me not to let it kick me in the ass, on the way out. He really thought I would be back, but I am happy to say I never returned. I went to live with a guy that I worked with at the auto stereo store.

It wasn't the best situation, but I knew I had to make it work. His mom charged me twenty-five dollars a month, gave me a room and fed me my meals. It was extremely gracious and generous of her. I remember how fond I was of sitting at the dinner table and looking into her kind eyes. She was a gentle soul, and she knew she was saving me from an extreme situation. My friend, on the other hand, had ulterior motives. I would find myself, yet again, in a precarious situation. I closed my eyes, told myself it was temporary, and focused my thoughts on what was going to be an illustrious future.

All of these scenarios propelled me forward with more passion toward my goal of going away to college. The applications were in and I was college bound.

CHAPTER 2

College Bound

The saving grace of acceptance
Its ritual and rites twist one's fate unto another
And the rejection again a tormented foe
The savior swept me aside and basked me in its
glory
As I lunged with fervor toward an unclaimed
story
Unraveled and ready for the new journey
Toward the great unknown

When it came to college applications, I was accepted to every school I applied for, but the paths were contradictory. It was a labyrinth of twists and turns, that made selecting a school that much more arduous. I have both a creative and a business side, which is fortuitous, but it's also a sort of relentless torture because I never know which direction to own. I love medicine and the tinctures that heal the body, I love performing, and enjoy arts and culture. I wasn't smart enough to figure out which career combined both elements, so I sat, divided for months, plotting out my unknown future, uncertain which direction to turn.

Stanford for Medicinal Arts, UCLA for Theater Arts, and every Ivy League school I could dream of decided that they wanted me at their school. I had very little savings, not even sure how I was going to make it through my first year, so UCLA was probably my most reliable bet. I accepted my fate and decided to attend the UCLA School of Theater. They accepted fifty people a year into the program, and I thought this was still prestigious, but it certainly wasn't like going to Stanford. Stanford was way too close to home, I needed to seek refuge much further away, so UCLA had won my spirit.

I graduated in 1982 as valedictorian of my high school, and everyone was there. Well, everyone except my parents; they somehow managed to skip out on the important tiers of my life. I accepted it for now and moved on. I am sure there was some cognitive mental therapy I would have to do in the future, but for now, in this present moment, it just wasn't so bad.

I was leaving my past behind and creating an exhilarating new chapter that had never been written or documented, and the pages would soon unfold to tell an incredible story of life and love. Love wasn't sparse on graduation day. My speech coach, my employers, and my high school faculty were all there. As my voice rang loudly through the microphone, I left my stamp at Pioneer High School in San Jose, California.

After accepting the faculty scholarship, my vision blurred with the salty essence of the light tears that ran down my face. When I wrapped up my valedictorian speech, I had a clarity and better understanding that San Jose, California, had no place nor purpose for me. I would never return. Prior to arriving at the dorms at UCLA, I was a sports expert at the Bob Mathias Olympic Sports Camp, outside of Fresno, and taught swimming and trampoline for a summer before starting my college journey; that's where I met Lyle Timmerman.

Little Lyle Timmerman was six years old and a child of mine at camp. He stayed in my cabin and was privy to scary ghost stories at bedtime and cartoon voices that I would throw around to entertain the kids. He had a great passion for life, and he loved the waterfront and the pollywogs and frogs of the lake.

Several times, I would take him out to the lake to view the wildlife, and he sparkled with excitement as he began to hit the pollywogs and frogs with his oar, from the narrow rowboat we stole from the nearby shore. I quickly rowed backward and removed Lyle from doing any further damage, having no idea he would reap so much joy from tormenting these little creatures. However, such is the life of a six-year-old boy, discovering the world around him and trying to discern which part had value and which could be discarded.

I told Lyle a story about his beginnings, and that he began as a little pollywog too, and imagine if someone would have come along with an oar and ended his life. He somehow managed to understand my strange analogy, and from that moment onward, we were good friends. He never smashed the pollywogs and frogs again. To my amazement, Lyle Timmerman's father was Vice-Chancellor at UCLA, and this would play a pivotal role in my upcoming college journey.

Let's just say that nothing in life is a coincidence; I firmly believe that to this day. After camp was over, little Lyle spoke to his father about the fun counselor he had shared his summer with, and his father lined up a job for me at UCLA, in the Veterans/Disabled Services Center inside Murphy Hall, which was the administration building at UCLA. The department was called Special Services, and it was special, indeed.

Murphy Hall was the hub and center of the UCLA campus. It was buzzing with excitement as new students entered the campus, signed up for classes and paid for enrollment. Murphy Hall was a destination for every student that attended UCLA and it would be my primary workplace for the next four years. I had packed one bag and took a greyhound bus, to fulfill my dreams in Los Angeles. I could barely contain my zeal and excitement as my abusive past slipped away. I would soon be transformed and in a safe environment, where I could focus on a brightly lit future. College was a financial struggle, as I knew it would be, and it became worse quarter after quarter. Eventually, I had no backup plan and wasn't sure I would make it through the following year. Remember that coincidence is purposeful, never accidental, as I segue back to Special Services.

Inside Special Services I worked across the desk from Shirley. Shirley had the best attitude, but you didn't want to cross paths with her. You could tell she had a hard life, but her eyes sparkled with a sense of hope as she followed God and walked a strong Christian path, full of light and love.

Shirley would occasionally share Scripture with me. One of her favorite quotes was an impactful piece of Scripture from I Corinthians 13: 4-6 about love: *"Love is patient, love is kind. It does not envy, it does not boast, it is not proud. It is not rude, it is not self-seeking, it is not easily angered, it keeps no record of wrongs. Love does not delight in evil but rejoices with the truth".* Shirley had a wisdom and understanding that completely attracted me, and I knew she was someone trustworthy and dependable - once she decided you belonged in her inner circle.

She was quite pretty, and I was attracted to her chocolate skin and genuine tenderness, as she went out of her way to provide motherly advice. She nurtured a sincere friendship that I regarded as priceless. Shirley altered my life one day in an unimaginable way and, of course Lyle Timmerman Senior, was the key catalyst. I worked in Veterans Affairs and Disabled Services, and veterans would come in to get their fees waived, as their college was paid for, due to their admirable service. I began to ask questions about the veterans. I remember my dad served in Vietnam, and he was one hundred percent disabled when he was discharged from the service.

Shirley lit up and explained that I might be entitled to the same benefits as the other veterans. I stood up in disbelief and listened, as Shirley stated that my college could be entirely paid for, if my dad was indeed one hundred percent disabled and honorably discharged from his service. I quickly filed the application, and sure enough, my dad was in that category upon being discharged. I was entitled to have my entire college tuition paid for, because I attended a state-run school. All of this alignment was overwhelming. It went all the way back to the Bob Mathias Sports Camp and little Lyle Timmerman.

I thanked God, immensely, that I didn't go to one of those Ivy League schools because none of the benefits were applicable if I had attended a private university. So here I was, sitting across from Shirley, when I heard the news. Everything I had paid for would be refunded to me. Not only would I receive tuition reimbursement, but I would receive three hundred and forty-two dollars every month for books as well.

Such a powerful and timely blessing, as God

placed me in the department at Murphy Hall, and it would vastly alter my ability to graduate, and it was the Bob Mathias Sports Camp that started it all. Nothing is a coincidence indeed. Let's not forget that!

Many of you may be questioning why my father was one hundred percent disabled from the service. The strep virus infiltrated his system while being employed in the Army, and in those days they pumped you intravenously with antibiotics. Sadly, this pump allowed the strep virus to move into his kidneys, and they literally ate his kidneys. He was on dialysis after renal failure and excused from service. He sadly died at the extremely young age of sixty, as no more of his collapsed veins could hold the dialysis needles he desperately needed in order to stay alive.

Even sadder, I found out before my dad passed, that he gave my mother critical college information. He told her that, if I attended a state school, my college would be paid for. My mother never gave me that critical information. Was it sabotage? Did my mother want me to fail, or did she really not remember?

We will never know, but I do think that jealousy played an intrinsic role, and for some strange reason my mother wanted to see me fail. Perhaps she was jealous that I was getting out to make a life for myself, and she felt she had none. Regardless, it was critical information I needed prior to applying for colleges. Those college applications were expensive, and I could have saved a few hundred dollars, which could have gone toward books or dorm fees had I applied only to state schools.

The good news is that God does align with us to make amazing things happen, and my working at Murphy Hall was indeed an amazing alignment. I am forever grateful that my entire university education was completely paid for, and I highly doubt I would have ever finished if it weren't.

Being a theater major was a taxing feat at best, and I found myself up at 7:00 a.m. each morning and going to bed after midnight for four years straight. I wanted to finish in four years, so I attended each summer school until completion. I was anxious to get out into the real world and get a taste of its offerings.

The theater curriculum was vast and consisted of classes, lectures, and then assisting the theater productions during our non-class time so that the productions could thrive. We were responsible for lighting, costuming, scenery, and everything that would go into a successful theatrical production. One either acted in a production or worked behind the scenes. I found myself enjoying the stage, and rehearsed, auditioned, and acted for many major UCLA productions. This is where I met future television star Mariska Hargitay.

Mariska and I would cross paths, being in the same major, and she invited a few of us to her house one day. She lived in the Hollywood Hills, and her house was a typical Hollywood mansion equipped with its own elevator to transport you between floors. I remember being thoroughly impressed with her wealth and status. I fantasized about having her life and living in a similar palace someday.

We spoke in great detail about her background, and she rarely revealed to anyone that she was Jayne Mansfield's daughter. I didn't know that at the time, nor did I know much about her father, Mickey Hargitay, an actor and famous bodybuilder. They were an elite, famous Hollywood couple, and Mariska was on the fence about announcing it to the world that she was indeed the daughter that survived that infamous car accident that sad day on June 29, 1967. She enjoyed a humble existence just being one of the gang at UCLA and hid behind a life she refused to cash in on, unless absolutely necessary.

She had a difficult time, as we all did, roping in a theatrical agent. I remember the moment when she finally decided to use her mother's name to garner an elite theatrical agent; she felt it was time to let the world know about her past. She released her little secret and enjoyed the cathartic journey of slowly opening Pandora's box. This brave step forward would place her center stage, directly in the spotlight, and this would be the last day we saw our Mariska Hargitay.

She started on *Falcon Crest* shortly after her announcement, and most of us never saw her again. She was a joy to be around, and I remember her showing me the scar on her forehead from the car accident that decapitated her mother. Her entire life seemed like a movie, so it was only appropriate that she continue in the footsteps of her esteemed mother and father. She was a lovely soul, and I am honored that I could spend some quality time swapping stories, although I felt hers were always a bit more interesting than mine.

I met many influential people, as most do in a university setting, but the most influential were those that I met at the Department of Special Services. Some were blind, while others had cerebral palsy or were wheelchair bound. There was a large variety of special needs individuals, but those that were visually impaired intrigued me the most, as they traversed across campus with a trailing cane and memorized landmarks, having no visual acuity at all. I would give tours to help them trail from class to class and call out specific landmarks that heightened their mental cognition, so they wouldn't end up lost on campus amongst the masses.

These people were strong spirited, and they had a clarity and focus I had never seen before. Many would argue that I had extreme determination and focus to get into college, but admittedly these people at Special Services were far beyond my comprehension. They would teach me valuable lessons about myself and my greater potential. I enjoyed and bonded with many of the Special Services students, but I learned the most from the visually impaired and those with cerebral palsy. We connected on a visceral level, and I finally decided to jump in, full steam, during the summer of 1983. I moved in with Chad, Richard, and Leiman. Chad and Richard were legally blind, and Leiman was visually impaired. I had certain responsibilities in the household that would include helping them sift through and read the mail. I recorded textbooks on tape both at home and at Special Services. Richard, in turn, taught me how to iron, and Chad and I would have long talks about life, its challenges, and which goals he was pursuing to complete his circle.

Chad and Richard always conspired to work together, and they were working on starting their own company while attending UCLA. Leiman was African-American and albino, and I had never seen this combination before. He would talk about women mostly, and I could tell there was this little empty space inside of him, that he needed filled. We had a few in-depth talks, but he loved to walk around naked. He would just sit there naked, which was slightly awkward. I think he was proud of what God had given him, and he wanted to show it to the world.

One beautiful, balmy summer evening all three of them approached me with a request. They wanted to see the new *Star Wars* movie, *Return of the Jedi*. I was extremely curious how we were all going to participate in this movie-going activity. Chad explained that I would interpret the entire film while we were all watching it, which included every sound effect, every living creature, and every crash and burn scenario that the movie could possibly generate. The theater was going to be packed, as it was the second day of the movie release, and I was concerned about the people around us. They would be disturbed by my interpreting the entire film, in an audible pitch, for my three friends to grasp.

The adventure was sure to stretch my imagination; I grabbed Chad on one arm, Richard on the other, and Leiman held the back of my coat as we ventured off to the theater. We arrived after a short jaunt on the neighborhood bus and onward into Westwood Village, then funneled in and took our seats. I should have reached out to the surrounding guests in our area, warning them that I would be translating the film for my friends, but the thought didn't occur to me until the lights went dim and the slanted credits began to role toward the top of the screen.

The audience clamored with excitement as the soundtrack bellowed throughout the entire theater. The woofers and subwoofers carried the music in Dolby Surround Sound to every audible speaker. The warships came into view, along with the Death Star, and my tongue began to translate every shape, color, sound effect, character, including the details of Darth Vader's costume, the shape of his helmet, and why he was making a strange breathing sound through his manmade breathing apparatus.

I had no idea that my vocal descriptors were no match for the visual acuity of this film, but I did my best to trudge forward to delight my friends as they listened intently to my every word. Sadly, the guests around me were also listening to my every word, and every few seconds I would get a loud "shush" or "be quiet," or "do you mind?" I retorted back that I did mind, my friends are blind, I am translating the film for them, and I am sorry but this will continue for the entire film; you are more than welcome to see the manager and get a refund to view the film on another day.

Chad and Richard laughed loudly at my response, and we continued to enjoy the film. My tongue swiftly described the next character on screen, which was the Jedi himself, Master Yoda, and I included his long animal-like ears, his matted green color and eyes that glowed with a century of wisdom.

Richard was born blind, and he had never seen color, and I knew that I would have to address the color issue later, but there was no time to dive into the semantics of color at that moment. The action was dynamic, and it was exhausting trying to keep up with the pace of the movie and ensure my friends understood the premise.

The end was most difficult as Darth Vader removed his mask, and it was my job to describe his face, as this was the first reveal of Mr. Vader. I stumbled through Humpty Dumpty stories and soon realized this analogy wasn't resonating at all. I compared his head to that of an egg, with a few strands of hair sticking out, and this seemed to provide some additional clarity as Darth Vader said goodbye to his son sharing one last loving moment on screen before he passed. The credits finally scrolled by, and my jaw was relieved to take a break from yapping. I sat in my chair, languidly, refusing to move a muscle. It was such an incredible journey with my three friends that summer. They instilled my spirit with admiration and humility.

I am grateful for being able to experience such an enlightened journey, being around individuals that lived in a world with no limitations. The outsider purveyed their world as a map filled with roadblocks and insurmountable obstacles, yet they simply had a few inconveniences they needed to overcome. Their refreshing approach to living was an insightful gift for those that took a sturdy gaze to digest it. I loved that summer, filling up my spiritual fuel tank. I would never forget my Three Musketeers, who showed me life through a different set of lenses, Sir Chad, Richard and Sir Leiman.

During that same summer, a petite woman named Darlene Bubis ventured into Special Services on account that she needed a few van rides punctually scheduled to transport her to her classes on time. Darlene had cerebral palsy, and like many others, it was a minor inconvenience for her and nothing more. She had an incredible sweetness about her - her blue eyes transfixed mine, with such purity and innocence, I was immediately attracted. After a few visits at Special Services, the two of us became quite flirtatious, and I finally mustered up the courage to ask her out.

Darlene was the epitome of humility. I was on the other side of the spectrum, as I admired her contentedness with life and the journey that was unfolding for her. I had a weakness for those pure spirits, those that left manipulation and deceit behind to live an honest and truthful existence. Their soul had nothing to hide. I looked forward to my date with Darlene and was hopeful that she too was feeling a genuine connection.

Date night Friday finally arrived, as Darlene and I ventured out to explore our world together. Our plan incorporated dinner and a movie, so I took her to Acapulco's, a Mexican restaurant in Westwood Village, close to the Avco, where we were going to see our film. Dinner came and went. We were both wearing half of our dinner on our shirts, but we didn't care too much, as we laughed throughout the meal. We devoured two orders of guacamole and fajitas, which were enough to feed nine families and their small children.

On our way up the Avco steps, Darlene stumbled, and I tried to catch her, and we both fell several stairs downward toward the bottom of the initial staircase. Her glasses were humorously twisted on her face, and we both sat at the bottom of the stairs and just giggled. Our connection was genuine as we sat together, still laughing, as I held her glasses in my hands, feverishly trying to get them back in some semblance of alignment. We were somehow light together, and the world just wasn't as heavy when we were hanging out. I continued to date Darlene for a while, and her parents wanted to know and understand my intentions, as I would frequently visit her house in Los Angeles where her folks also resided. I didn't know my intentions, as I didn't even know myself at this point, so how could I answer such a question? I was a soul that was searching for happiness but the term eluded me, altogether.

I do feel that her parents had every right to understand my intention. They were protecting their daughter from being hurt, if I wasn't serious about my feelings towards her. I felt it was a little soon to have that conversation, and it scared me away from enjoying any future adventures with my sweet Darlene. We are good friends, to this day, and she is happily married, doing well, as I knew she would.

College was a transformative time for me, and theater was a tough major. I was a soft spirit, and if I were going to pursue the motion picture business or theater, I needed to toughen up. Delia Salvi was the most prominent acting coach at UCLA, and she coached many of the MFAs (Master of Fine Arts), but she did teach one intro class in acting. We all had to audition for that class in hopes that we would be accepted. If anyone could toughen up a soft spirit, it would be Ms. Salvi.

Delia loved her job, but more than anything she loved to destroy the little blonde sorority girls during their heartfelt auditions, while they tried to understand characterization, and reinterpret the character's emotional scale. The scenario was always the same: Each sorority girl would begin the first sentence of their monologue, and Delia would interrupt them and ask them how they are feeling. They would always answer back with "What do you mean?" and Delia would laugh and say, "Exactly." "There is nothing going on here, and if you can't give me more than that then just get out." The girls would try to muster up their courage to continue, Delia would scream, "Get out!," and many of them would be so flustered, with papers flying in the air, that they would depart, crawling out of class, picking sides up, along the way.

For those not in the business, 'sides' are small scripts, used for auditions, and are usually given to us prior to a casting call. Delia had a great deal of fun in class and, wanting to be admitted, needing the growth, I was prepared to answer her questions with the utmost authenticity. I didn't want to end up crawling out of class, sobbing, as many did in the past.

My name was called, and I rose to the musty stage, choosing to audition with a scene rather than a monologue, utilizing another female partner who was a friend of mine, also a theater major. In the middle of the scene, Delia interrupted me, screaming that I am safe, not vulnerable, and nothing is happening. She somehow knew how to climb inside my head, which started to trigger me emotionally, so I yelled back at her with a hard snap in my voice, and she told me to use it in the scene. I turned around and slapped my audition partner so hard across the face that she fell to the ground in disbelief. Delia applauded and was thrilled to see some spontaneous combustion fill the room. I was ultimately accepted to Ms. Salvi's class. She was a tough woman, and she really prepared us for the vicious and cruel outside world of moviemaking. I am forever in her debt.

She passed away in March 2015, and I will always carry a piece of her soul with me. She taught me how to survive in the movie business and was truly gracious and kind. She was all bark and no bite; I enjoyed her presence very much. I am sure she is missed by so many that she inspired.

Speaking of sorority girls, as we depart from Delia's thrashing adventures, there was one that caught my eye. I ended up dating her the last three years of college. Her spirit emitted so much light that sometimes, it was hard to look at her without slipping on my sunglasses, just to get a good view. She was simple, pure, and much like a golden retriever, she was as loyal as any dog I knew, and dogs were my eternal weakness. I loved her, and we grew together in spirit, creating extraordinary memories that would swoon even the most jaded socialite. She had the thickest, long blonde hair, emerald green eyes, and a voice that could lull even the most difficult infant to sleep. She was an actress, a strong singer, and her voice mirrored that of the Disney classic ingénue, *The Little Mermaid*.

Weekends with Linda would include jaunts to the world-famous Beverly Hills Hotel, where she knew one of the piano players inside the Polo Lounge. Antonio and Linda would sing duets side by side while we sipped on White Russians, Midori, and Chambord. The walls were draped with painted green tropical palms leaves as was the motif and style of the hotel, and each section of the lounge's dimly lit tables accompanied a flickering votive. The Polo Lounge was notorious for serving guests under the age of twenty-one during the eighties. The Lounge had a strict dress code and guests who didn't sport a coat and tie could rent them at their coat check for a nominal fee, or they would be denied entry.

It was the perfect night out for Linda and I. We sipped on expensive Chambord and pretended we were Hollywood royalty, living out our fantasies alongside the real rich and famous. During the 80's, The Polo Lounge attracted an elite group of socialites, and it was only appropriate that two starving students, who dreamed of being celebrities, would hobnob right alongside them. Naturally, we couldn't afford to go there often, but when we did, we fit right in.

Linda's voice soothed the audience while singing a few numbers, leaning against Antonio's piano. Somehow, in our little minds, we felt we had become actual celebrities ourselves simply by association. The fantasy was intoxicating, and

Dave El Limousine service always escorted us back to the UCLA campus for free, compliments of The Polo Lounge. It was always fun to arrive back to campus in a black stretch limo, while the other students looked in bewilderment, wondering how we could afford such luxurious evenings.

It was all a façade, but to Linda and me it was a fairy tale adventure that we wouldn't easily give up. Dating a sorority girl also meant countless invitations to parties, one of them being the esteemed Spring Ball at the illustrious and posh Bel Air Hotel. The small bridge divided the pond from the entrance of the hotel and was decorated with black-and-white swans. Its reflection sifted downstream and provided the perfect backdrop for this black-tie event. Linda and I loved to dress in our finery, and we knew this occasion would highlight our love for that lifestyle. We loved the fantasy of the Disney movies and found ourselves elated when we could create those moments in real life.

During the ball, we took a stroll outside and stumbled upon a gazebo, right near the pond where the swans were waddling by. Linda looked at me playfully and said, "Look, a gazebo just like the one in *The Sound of Music*." She winked, didn't miss a beat, and broke into song as I interrupted her and explained that Rolfe starts the scene in "I am sixteen going on seventeen,". I then broke into song as, I grabbed her hand and lifted her onto the bench inside the gazebo, reenacting the entire scene.

Even the weather seemed to cooperate as tiny droplets of perfect rain began to fall in the middle of Linda's scene, as she split leaped over the benches in her ball gown. We laughed and held each other, kissing amongst the swans and finery of the Bel Air Hotel. It was a perfect moment, and even though perfection is impossible to define, this moment was rich with its refined backdrop, even better with the two souls that intertwined and danced about with joy.

We shared many joyous adventures inside mansions, yachts, and dinner parties with her sorority friends. Linda and I had a special connection, destined to live our lives together, or so I thought. I was confused throughout college, and I would push people away, afraid to transpose the story onto my final book called *My Life,* always feeling that somehow it could be better than the one I was living.

I did this thousands of times in my life, and sadly I did it to Linda too. I left a spear inside her heart that would never heal. I always carried a bit of guilt about the fact that I wanted to see the world and taste it fully, whatever that meant, and I left love behind, choosing emptiness over the richness it provided.

Linda never really understood, and perhaps I never really valued a real love situation, not understanding how rare it was. Years later Linda and I connected on Facebook, exchanged numbers and called each other one evening. She had a slew of questions for me and was still feeling insecure about my decision to move on with my life without her. Linda told me she never married; I asked her why.

She kept quiet for a moment, I could tell she was having difficulty getting out the words, and then she said it, "No one wanted to dance with me in the rain." My eyes started to well up a bit, and I understood her completely. Our love was unique, and it would always be difficult to compare our love with another. I was hoping she would be able to move on and not compare but embrace something new; I believed she could create some new memories, that were just as rich and beautiful. I didn't understand these vital substances until much later in my life, but for the moment, I was to carry the burden of Linda's life being incomplete.

It was graduation day, and like other graduation days in my past, my parents were nowhere to be found. I spent the day with Linda's family, and it was gracious of them to include me inside their inner circle. Graduation was here, and it was a milestone that had finally passed. I was anxious to get out into the real world and leave my mark. Her family treated me like one of their own, and the day was as delightful as it could be considering my family was invisible. Linda was always there for me, her spirit bright and full of light, as always.

It's rare to understand value, how to cherish it when we have nothing to compare it to, and have minimal life experience. Our minds are constantly living in the future, or visiting the past, and our present moment seems to disappear amongst our mindless chatter, which drags us from one subject to the next. I was very much a prisoner of my mind, and I simply didn't know any better. I didn't know how to live in the present, and I certainly didn't know the meaning of value and how to embrace it.

I was young, immature, and lost. I was fulfilling a dream, while hurting others along the way- but what was the dream really about? No deep impactful questions were being asked; I just followed this path, assuming happiness would align with me along the way. I am not even sure I understood at that moment what happiness was or what it truly meant. I had glimpses or moments of it, but I kept leaving it behind for some future thing I was chasing, that would ultimately bring me more happiness.

Inevitably, I would chase happiness for decades, and I would leave so many happy scenarios behind to chase some future happiness. I didn't understand the definition of happiness and what it meant, so I would continue chasing a wispy phantom into an unknown world that wasn't equipped to provide me with the happiness I sought. Without understanding what we seek, we are on a future road that fervently propels us forward but rarely aligns us with our desired happiness and spiritual fulfillment. If I didn't understand the definition of happiness, how would I know when it arrived?

I knew I needed to acknowledge the present or it would slip by as an ignored flower on my deck side porch that I failed to see every morning; thus its beauty is nonexistent. My parochial vision left me stranded on a black-and-white island, while others lived on the same island, but enjoyed it in color. I believe this to be the case with Linda, as I didn't understand the beauty staring back at me. I was living in the future, and so my present moments with Linda would disappear, as if they were never born to provide me with any sense of pleasure.

My college years were gone, and so was Linda. The real world was here, I was about to embark on my greatest journey and feel the world's power as I was tossed about, like a speed ball in an Ivy League lacrosse tournament. The real world was something I was not prepared for, but out I went to seek my fortune and my identity. Little did I know that I already had both, but for now it was a void in my mind and spirit. I needed to go on this journey and be pummeled by this thing called "Life". The hardened exterior of my soul needed to be broken so the tiny cracks and fissures could share some emergence of light.

CHAPTER 3

The Hollywood Shuffle

The void inside me sings a melancholy song
As I move through the journey of someone else's
dictation
And am bossed and tossed about like a buoy on a
vociferous sea
I break away from the flock, and plunge into the
eclipsed night
Not knowing where or when someone
will save me
It is then during this silence and loneliness
The chatter gone
That clarity begins to seep through the pores of
my skin
And it is here that I find myself for the first time

I t was 1986, and I was anxious to find an agent and get started. Acting was my business, and I was my own product. I visited Samuel French on Sunset Blvd., based on some friend's feedback and picked up the current agent listing. I sent my eight-by-ten headshots to some reputable agents, hoping they would leave a message with my answering service or machine. Many agents listed in the guide, would refuse unsolicited submissions. This encouraged me further to barrage them with my eight-by-ten glossies. Commercial agents were easy to obtain, and they focused solely on commercial auditions, commercial print, and voiceover work.

Theatrical agents were much pickier and more selective as their reputation depended on their roster of clients nailing their auditions with the top-tier casting directors in town. It was an extremely competitive business, selfishly aligned with the romantic narcissist that would do anything to become a star.

A few weeks passed after sending out my submissions, I received my first voicemail message from Cunningham, Escott and Dipene (CED) in Beverly Hills. Cunningham is an "A" list agent and still represents some of the most expensive talent in town. I was nervous and excited to return the call and set up an interview with one of their commercial agents. I had no idea how to prepare, and all my actor friends advised me to be myself. I suppose that would have been great advice if I knew what it meant to "be myself," but I didn't, so I would flounder through a series of interviews, posing frozen, much like an ice sculpture sporting zero personality and inevitably impressing no one.

I arrived thirty minutes early at CED and was escorted into a large conference room that easily sat twenty-five people. I imagined this being the boardroom where careers were made while others were swiftly decapitated. The agent entered the room and literally sat twenty-five seats away from me, screaming her questions across the table. I thought to myself that a microphone would be a most appropriate tool at this given moment. I felt nausea welling up to a formidable climax in my stomach, as she continued screaming from across the room, asking me for my credentials.

I couldn't communicate intimately with someone seated so far away, and I am not sure why I didn't just walk over and sit next to her. Perhaps that was the test, and I wasn't passing this one, as fear imprisoned me, and I was perpetually glued to my chair. She continued her drill and eventually her words became muffled as she transformed into a Charles Shultz character from the comic strip *Peanuts*.

Her words became inaudible and disenchanting as I sat their frozen in time. Fear's insipid grasp finished me that day, and I didn't have the appropriate tools to remove it. It simmered much like a potion bubbling inside a witch's brew as my anxiety escalated, and I was finally asked to leave.

I had several other auditions with other commercial and theatrical agents, but again fear was in my way, and I didn't understand how to sell myself and bring out my shimmering persona. The interview process became a black hole that sucked out my lifeforce and left me vacuous and depleted. I was stuck in my little galaxy of fear, and with the black hole within my reach, there was simply no escape.

I found an ad in *Dramalogue* for a commercial acting workshop with noted commercial actor Randy Kirby, and I signed up. *Dramalogue* was our version of *Backstage* in the eighties, and many acting coaches advertised in this popular paper publication.

Randy's workshop guaranteed a showcase video at the end of class that he shopped around to the top agents in town including William Morris. I was completely comfortable in front of other actors, and I excelled, but when it came to agents and casting directors or people of power, I simply embraced the fear zone. Randy shopped my final tape around and got me solid interviews with practically every incredible commercial agent in the city, and my confidence shifted a bit. I had a few decent interviews with a few agents and was able to read some sides and be creative. The fear began to subside.

I signed a deal with a top agent and started going out on some major commercial auditions. National commercials paid the most and were the most competitive, but I wasn't a member of the Screen Actors Guild (SAG) and you needed to have a SAG card in order to do union commercial work, so that would be a huge challenge. Luck was about to come my way, or should I say, an intentional coincidence was about to fall from the sky and land directly in my path.

Miller's Outpost was a popular clothing brand, much in the genre of Old Navy, and they were looking for extras for one of their commercial shoots. Extra work didn't pay that well, but it did allow others to see you on the set, and I figured I could make a good impression once I was on set performing.

My headshot was sent in, and I was selected. I arrived on set extremely early in the morning and sat around while the principal roles were being put in makeup and wardrobe. I remember feeling jealous and thinking to myself that I was just as good if not better than the principals. I didn't have much humility at this point in my life. I was subject to my superficial emotions, as I hadn't done much spiritual work other than work at a camp or do some service at UCLA.

I had a ton of work to do in that arena, and emotions such as jealousy and feeling superior were toxic emotions, harmful for me both physically and spiritually. Onward I went into a jealous stupor, plotting my way out of the extras table. I came up with an idea the following day as we changed locations to the beach in Santa Monica.

During my high school years I was a gymnast and one-meter springboard diver, and in this moment, this skillset was about to pay off in a major way. I ran down to the sand during our lunchbreak and began a round of back handsprings, followed by a series of backflips, relentless until someone of power came down to greet me. The director drug his feet through the sand and confronted me as I quickly finished a series of back handsprings ending with a layout backflip. He seemed inspired with my gymnastic ability and felt he could use a principal actor with this skillset the following day, as it would spice up some of the beach scenes.

Some call it luck, while others might say you were in the right place at the right time, but I am a firm believer that we can alter our outcome with some inspired thought and a little action. As a principal actor, I would be eligible for SAG, and wouldn't have any issues working on any union projects from that day forward. It was a pivotal moment for me, a moment we all wait for as actors.

I stayed present long enough to thank God as I looked toward the sky with gratitude and held a feeling inside my soul that could only be called happiness. It was momentary happiness, but happiness, nonetheless. I floated above the ground, enjoying the rest of the shoot that day, and I never touched the ground again for several weeks afterward.

Miller's Outpost contacted my agent several times that year, and I ended up being a principal actor for five or six more commercials the same year. Money was flowing in for the first time, but not enough to leave my waiting job behind, just enough to know that I was on the right track. My agent was happy, and this little bout of confidence catapulted me onto a soap opera called *Young and the Restless.* I landed a role on this soap as Scott, a drunken fool who eventually got the main character killed via alcoholism. I was only supposed to shoot for a couple of days, be introduced at a party, and then the role would end.

On soaps, if a role returns, we call it a recurring role, and if you are contracted for three years, then you have a contract role. Scott was a drunk on the show, and obviously this was a perfect fit for me, as I certainly did enjoy drinking my share on the weekends. It was an easy part, and I played it like a true drunk stumbling about and knocking Mrs. Chancellor (Jeannie Cooper) all over the set.

I was only supposed to shoot a couple of episodes, and then I would be wrapped and onto my next acting adventure. I went into wardrobe to get my fitting for the following day, and a good friend of mine from UCLA, Greg York, was head of wardrobe for *Y&R.* We had a lot of fun together reminiscing about our college days, and I was proud that he made it in the business with a regular gig. He was uber talented and deserved all the accolades he received, including a full-time gig as a costume designer.

A few people from CBS did see me on *Y&R* when the episodes aired a month later and some key executives were launching a new soap called *Bold and the Beautiful.* They contacted my agent and wanted me to screen test for a three-year contract role. *Y&R* decided not to release me, and they told *B&B* that I was recurring on *Y&R* and would not be available to be on their soap. This was interesting news to me because no one communicated any such thing, nor did they communicate anything to my agent. *Y&R* did end up using me a few more times that year, and that was it, so I was passed up for a three-year contract role for a few stints on *Y&R*, and all I can say is "That's Hollywood."

Shooting my last two episodes on *Y&R* would be life altering. I didn't know it at the time, but I was leaving on-camera work for good as my continual search for happiness tore me from one scenario to the next.

I remember sitting in the dressing room upstairs at CBS, and the Production Assistant arrived, informing me that the script had changed. He gave me my new lines, which needed to be memorized immediately, and slammed my door.

I was called on set, ran downstairs, and noticed the lighting was dim and poorly lit. I figured it must have something to do with the production budget. Nonetheless it was bothersome, and I thought it was time to use my UCLA theater degree, sauntered over to the lighting guy and engaged in conversation about side lighting and sprucing up the set with a few more robust lighting stands. To my surprise, he wasn't too receptive. He lightly slapped me on the face three times, told me to go over to my mark and stand there look pretty because that's what I was hired to do. It was extremely demoralizing, and I was starting to understand that the outside world wasn't so kind as I slunk up to my dressing room and sat down in front of the mirror. I drifted into the past remembering Delia Salvi's class and how I needed to toughen up. In that moment her words were deafening as I shifted from a state of gratitude to one of sadness and despair.

I didn't understand the real world at all, yet alone the intricacies of Hollywood, but God was sending me a strong message that day and it would be transformative. I sat there in my dressing room looking into the mirror, my eyes starting to tear up, as I was overtaken by an overwhelming sense of emptiness.

I had worked so hard to arrive at this point being a working actor; I had studied for four years in college and taken several acting classes. I prepared for this moment my entire life. If this work was a vacuous pit for me, then where would that leave me and where would I go? I sat there for a long time until I was called to the set to finish my last episode.

I couldn't shake the empty feeling away, and I knew I had to make a change. I didn't like being a pawn in a game where I had zero control, while the people in power told me who to be, where to stand, what to look like, and how to behave. The sense of fear crept back in as I had no other skillset and no other option for a career path, or so I thought. Leaving CBS that night, I knew I wouldn't return anytime soon. I knew I had some big decisions to make, life-altering decisions that would shape a different future than the one I had dreamed of my entire life.

The following day the feeling was the same. Empty, sad, and lifeless, I called my agent and explained my current plight. She selfishly told me to meditate or take a nap, and the feelings would subside. She had no real connection to my feelings or the deep, gut-wrenching sadness I was experiencing. I finished the phone call by firing her and proceeded to do the same with my commercial, voiceover, and print agent. The puppet festival was at a close. My puppet strings were no longer firm and rigid, but dangled loosely by my side, as I released them and the people that had pulled them so many times.

I was good at leaving everything behind, including my career, my relationships, and friendships. I was listening to that voice in my head that dictated my next move and informed me that the next corner would be filled with riches and happiness. One doesn't usually go from something to nothing, but apparently nothing sounded pretty good, at that moment, so off I went into nowhere land, with no plan and not much joy to propel me forward.

Thankfully I had my college degree in Theater/Motion Picture Television and lived in the entertainment capital of the world. The allure of the movie business was simmering inside my soul, but I wasn't enamored with being on camera, so perhaps playing a role behind the scenes would provide a stronger alignment. When I wasn't waiting tables, I was interning for free, because I needed to experience different environments to better understand where I wanted to fit inside the industry.

Most offices loved having a free intern fresh out of college, so off I went to several new adventures each week. I worked in casting and at a talent agency. Both were empty worlds for me, as most actors were treated so poorly. I wasn't sure I needed to be associated with acting at all, as it kept reminding me of that day inside my dressing room at CBS where I felt that strong ping of emptiness.

A friend of mine recommended an agency called "The Right Connections" that specialized in placing temps at the different motion picture studios around town. I set up an appointment, registered with the agency, took several tests. To my surprise, I did have skills such as a fast-and-accurate typing speed and some word processing skills. I interviewed with a recruiter at the agency, and several hours later I was receiving temp placement calls. It really was that easy.

Once I was placed, it was up to me to, not allow that fear zone to take over and replace the star I had silently hiding inside of me, or so I thought. I didn't know much about this hidden star, but it was about to burst forth and light the darkened tunnel I was slinking through, revealing a new road, a new path dimly lit with promise.

I told myself that the stakes weren't that high, as it seemed to lower my inner anxiety. I was able to shine and explore a multitude of entertainment opportunities. I worked in development, publicity, finance, and consumer products, while God and I conspired to build a career at the studios inside the consumer products division. This little adventure took a couple of years before I really understood where I wanted to be placed. Inside the Consumer Products Division, there was a Licensing Department, Marketing, Publicity, Finance, Sales, Retail and more. This division worked with other licensees to produce branded items based on movies and television shows that the studio owned and trademarked.

I figured being an assistant to an executive would be the best role, as my sponge-like brain could adapt to my new environment and learn the inner workings of the division. After temping for a Vice President of Licensing at Saban Entertainment for three months, I was finally offered a permanent position as an executive assistant. I felt a sense of belonging, and a camaraderie with the team at Saban. It was a comfortable place that was driven with passion, excitement, and opportunity.

Saban Entertainment was a young company of about twenty employees, which was about to change as the *Mighty Morphin Power Rangers* would alter its status and size forever, amassing four hundred plus employees, six months after I began my fulltime position at the company. I arrived on the ground floor of a growing studio, and the place was buzzing, as every licensee in the industry wanted a piece of the *Power Rangers*. It was a fast-paced environment and certainly not for everyone, but I loved it. I loved working quickly and having multiple projects to juggle all at once. Every few years executives rotated in and out of the studio or were fired as was the case with the vice president that I was assisting, and my position downgraded to that of assisting a Director of Licensing once she departed.

The job was extremely boring, and I didn't know how to be more proactive and create extra work for myself, so I sat there for about six months deciding whether I should leave, as I really didn't understand how to get out of the Assistant role and into something more challenging. I was good as an Assistant, so good, that no one wanted to see me leave the position, so I was never offered any promotions. With all of the movement and energy at Saban, it appeared I was stuck in a dead-end job.

I left my cube one day and knocked on the President's door to have a little chat with him, as his door was right outside my little cubicle, and he was an extremely approachable individual. His name was Peter, and I saw people walking in and out of his office all day, so I figured I could probably just pop my head in and say hi.

I knew he appreciated the job I did at Saban, and we seemed to have a good rapport. I looked in and asked him if he had a minute. He nodded as I closed the door behind me. I told him about the Assistant job and the simple tasks that were required as I yawned throughout my day until I was ready to clock out. I felt a piece of my soul dying, as I continued to explain my feelings and lack of motivation.

I will never forget his response, and I was amazed, surprised, and completely stupefied by what he had to say. He was obviously disappointed with me, and explained with conviction that Saban was a place that needed talented individuals to grow it; without this talent, the company would be buried in mediocrity with little chance of survival.

He stared at me for a few seconds and said he would accept my resignation if I felt I had no more to offer, or I could write out a job description where I could impact the company vision, taking the boredom of my current position and turn it into something meaningful. I looked at him blankly for a moment, then with a small gleam in my eye, I began to understand his wisdom and the purpose of our little chat together, as he asked me to get out of his office and kindly close the door.

I returned to my cube, and I wasn't sure exactly what he meant, but it sounded like he wanted me to create my own position, a job that would have strong alignment with my skillset and help the company grow. I knew enough to understand that this was a *carpe diem* moment, and within one hour I handed him a fifteen-page document outlining my new job description. I had little to do outside of answering the phone or scheduling a meeting, so whipping out my future took very little time, as time wasn't a factor in my current position. Peter understood the cindering fire I had burning inside, he held the keys to the castle and the power to change my life within the doors at Saban. This was just the beginning of his tutelage, mentorship, and unconditional friendship that I would be blessed to experience while working under his leadership.

Less than twenty-four hours later Peter called me in his office, told me my position was approved, and returned my fifteen-page document. He wished me luck, smiling, as he told me to get out of his office. Before I left, he explained that the office next door to him was open, and I was to move my things, begin my new position immediately, and he would let the Director of Licensing know that I had been promoted.

I packed up my desk, which took minutes to accomplish, and entered my first office as a Manager of Licensee Relations, working for a studio that represented the billion-dollar franchise: The *Mighty Morphin Power Rangers*. I sat down and unfolded my job description. It was vast and intimidating, and I was proud that I didn't walk away this time. I broke the pattern as I intellectually maneuvered, with the help of Peter, into my new role and new life at Saban.

My core responsibility as a new manager was building relationships with the licensees to ensure they were getting approvals on time, assist them with the style guide process, and become their liaison within the organization. Saban had grown so fast that the communication was delicately frayed, and it was my job to sync a tighter communication tether with the licensees. These top tier licensees produced successful licensed products worldwide and building relationships with them meant career stability and job security. Each day meant millions of dollars for our licensees, so approvals and retail communication were critical as they rushed their products onto store shelves in time for Q4 - which in toy land is holiday season.

I was juggling a million projects at once and I couldn't have been happier. There were *Mighty Morphin Power Ranger* tours, appearances, trade shows, and industry events such as Toy Fair and Licensing Show. I wanted to do it all, but specifically I enjoyed helping with the events and putting together the industry shows and press conferences. I learned that I had a keen eye for detail, or so I was told, and had strong memory retention.

I would find out later that these skills were a direct requirement if you wanted to become a successful event planner. I didn't know much about events at this point, but I knew that I was excited about them, and I wanted to attend every soiree possible.

One of the glitziest and star-studded events that Saban participated in was NATPE. The National Association of Television Program Executives (NATPE) was a distribution show and celebrity affair, as tradeshow booths exceeded one million dollars in production costs. The dinners were elegant, and the clients were savvy entrepreneurs with deep pockets, and I was soon immersed in a world that mesmerized me. I had the entertainment bug, and I had it bad.

The event world was exhilarating, and Peter lined up more projects for me, which included flying to Mexico City to help launch *Power Rangers* worldwide. I spoke Spanish and had some production experience, so I would have a dual role to introduce Peter on stage in Spanish and then run to the booth to cue up the videos for the presentation. We didn't have CDs or digital playback, so the program had to be produced and thrown on the screen by hand. The booth provided many sweat-filled moments as I ran from queue to queue syncing the presentation to the precise moment when each slide or video was needed on screen.

The show launch went well, and Peter always had a unique way of thanking his team, as he bowed and said goodnight. He had a white stretch limo at his disposal afterward, but explained that he was tired, and the Manager of Events, Marlene Cuesta, and I could use it for the night and enjoy a nice dinner at Valentina's. Valentina's was a five-star restaurant in the Zona Rosa area of Mexico City, and the service and food were Michelin star. Shortly after arriving at the restaurant, Marlene was craving a cigarette and as she pulled one out of her case, a bus boy ran toward her and slid approximately thirty feet and swooped in to light her cigarette. Our five-star dinner was well underway as Marlene happily puffed on her Newport Menthol's, and the menus and black napkins magically landed on our laps and tabletops respectively. The stemware floated to our right as the glimmer of several sets of silver sparkled beneath the shadow of the wine glass, which spilled over the table and danced about under the candlelight.

Unbeknownst to us, Peter held our dinner reservation with his credit card, and we enjoyed a Michelin star experience without a bill being presented at the end of the evening, and a limo scurried us back to the hotel. I would learn that Peter was an expert at creating priceless memories, but most important to me, was the dopamine effect of working hard and being handsomely rewarded.

That's just how he rolled. Peter valued his team, and through actions, he buried us with his eternal appreciation. His mentorship inspired me to be a more gracious person. I would soon find myself in the future, leading by his example, as great leaders leave an indelible mark. I tried my best to fill the shoes of this great man every moment I could seize an opportunity.

We returned from Mexico City as licensing heroes, or at least that's the way Peter made us feel. We had launched *Power Rangers* worldwide, and the licensing community in Mexico was ravenous. We had interest from some of the greatest manufacturers in the city. I imagine

Haim was also pleased, as his company became the focal point of Hollywood, his *Mighty Morphin Power Rangers* would literally take over the licensing world. Every elite manufacturer wanted a taste of the *Power Rangers*, and they were willing to pay almost anything to get it. It's rare in Hollywood when a studio is in such a fortuitous position, and Saban Entertainment's *Power Rangers* were on its way to becoming a billion-dollar franchise.

A year moved swiftly in my newly created position at Saban, the projects kept pouring in and I embraced each one with enthusiasm and an inexplicable excitement. One afternoon Peter knocked on my door and asked me to come into the conference room for a brief meeting. He had a strange smirk on his face, and I wasn't sure what was happening, but I trusted Peter with my life.

I was so loyal under his tutelage and leadership that, if he asked me to fly to China to buy him a red silk scarf, and it was important to him, I certainly would have done it - no questions asked. I assumed he had some new top-secret project he wanted me to handle, and I was already mentally churning about the prospects.

I entered the conference room, and to my utter surprise all the top executives were seated as several bottles of champagne were chilling on ice. Peter asked me to take a glass of champagne, and toast.

I asked what we were toasting to, and he said, "We are toasting to you." At that moment he pulled out this glass award showcasing the Saban Children's Entertainment Group logo, and the words "President's Award for Outstanding Achievement," with my name at the bottom. I tried to formulate some semblance of a sentence, but I found myself speechless as I swallowed my champagne to conceal my nervousness, the entire executive team clapped and toasted to me.

To think, one year prior, I was ready to depart. Peter planted the seed of inspiration and gave a selfless and tremendous gift for which I am forever thankful. Knowing oneself is critical, and without this reflected gauge, we're liable to make the wrong decisions, allowing ourselves to be treated poorly or disrespectfully by the entertainment bullies of the world. Some might even call it self-sabotage when we continue to walk away or run from a situation without the confidence or knowledge to confront our fear and stuff it back inside Pandora's Box for eternity.

My sense of self was growing, and my skillset was unfolding to further define my career, but sadly no further at Saban. Peter left and was off to run Sony Signatures, whose name would rebrand into Sony Pictures Consumer Products. I would be jobless as the new Vice President of Licensing arrived at Saban and hired her friends from Disney. The entertainment industry was very capricious, to say the least.

Two weeks after receiving the prestigious President's Award, I was laid off from Saban Entertainment and had to say goodbye to my illustrious *Power Rangers* and the brand that I helped build. "That's entertainment!"

A few months passed, when my illustrious leader gave me a call to tell me he might have an opportunity at Sony Pictures Consumer Products (SPCP). According to Peter, an executive in marketing was going on maternity leave. He wanted me to step in for a short period of time to keep the flow going and try to build something meaningful. I remember he was very clear about not being able to offer me anything permanent, but I should probably embrace it and we could revisit things once the executive returned from her leave. I enthusiastically said "yes," and he told me to start the next morning with some further instructions of how to park on the studio lot and where to report.

SPCP was the licensing arm of Columbia/TriStar Pictures, and it encompassed both the film and television divisions. This meant that we would provide licensing opportunities for all feature films as well as television properties. These included *I Dream of Jeannie, Wheel of Fortune*, and *Jeopardy.*

I drove in the next morning and was greeted at the gate by a guard who directed me to where to park and checked my name off his padded, white tablet. I entered the TriStar Building and was greeted by two more guards who had me check in and directed me toward the SPCP Department. I arrived at Peter's office, and he briefly showed me around and escorted me to the marketing department, where I would stay temporarily, waiting patiently for further instructions. I distinctly remember the energy being vastly different than Saban, and there was an air of sophistication and intimidation at a studio this size. People dressed to impress, and celebrities would come and go from the TriStar Building meeting with the President of Worldwide Marketing since his office was in the same building as ours. Deals were being made, real deals that would shape the motion picture business of tomorrow.

Saban felt more like a family environment where we protected each other from the unpredictability of the business. This one made me feel very vulnerable as an energy of uncomfortability filled the space. I needed all protective faculties on high alert, but I wasn't sure how to accomplish this as my spiritual component was less evolved and my mind was currently running the show. I walked toward the entryway. There were several display cases, highlighting a handful of popular intellectual properties and key consumer products, including an extra-large Wheel of Fortune slot machine.

Peter intercepted me in the entryway and asked me to deliver some important correspondence to a key executive in the Thalberg Building. He wanted me to understand the studio layout including the buildings where the key players resided. The Thalberg building was a cart ride down from ours, and the lobby was adorned with palatial art deco glass and black and white checkered floors as a gold line of Academy Awards glistened in crystal display cases, the sunlight breaking through onto the art deco glass. They stood as royal figures waiting for everyone to acquiesce and bow before them.

In between the two buildings was an executive dining room, The Rita Hayworth, where Director level and above could dine at lunch to woo their potential business partners. Live shows and principal photography for feature films were being shot at the various sound stages sporadically placed around the lot perimeter.

Some stage doors were open to reveal the magic unfolding inside. It was a thrilling place, but also an intimidating one, and once again I didn't feel good enough. Returning to my office, both a bit timid and unsure, I sifted through some paperwork and invoices and tried to soak in the responsibilities of my executive temp position. I knew I was a solid relationship builder and thought it would be beneficial to visit some of the offices, say hello, learn about the premier licenses and get a pulse on which materials could be created to make the selling process easier.

The top tier licensees from Saban, would be the same people vying for licenses at SPCP, and this thought provided me with a bit of momentary peace as I moved throughout my day. I figured if I was going to be there for the short term, I could play a vital role as a marketing services person provide video, and collateral materials that sales could use to sell in SPCP's properties. The studio had the *Men in Black* franchise as well as *Godzilla, Charlie's Angels, Stuart Little,* and *Spider-Man* to name a few.

I was there for about a week when Peter called me into his office with some news. The executive that was on leave sadly had a stillborn pregnancy; she was returning to work almost immediately. I understood, and thanked him for the opportunity, but he said he wasn't finished. He needed me to give him more time, and while he was sorting out other matters, he wanted me to continue with my marketing services role and branch into a full event role, but he needed to get approval from the studio.

I told him I didn't want him to feel pressured about securing a position for me, but he silenced me with the wave of his hand and I knew that meant our meeting was over. Within a few hours Peter magically secured approval from the SVP of Worldwide Marketing, which was his direct report, and I would now be part of the permanent SPCP Team as the Director of Marketing Services and Special Events reporting to the VP of Marketing.

It was certainly a day to celebrate, but the worry and insecurity of my own mind chatter imprisoned my celebration and turned to defacing my own self-worth, worrying about my uncertain future. If I was going to survive in this environment, I needed to understand myself and get rid of the negative chatter in my head. My sense of vulnerability and insecurity would open a gateway to some inspiration, which would provide some clarity and guidance for my new journey at Sony. There were several great speakers and seminars about being present, and a few were recommended by my fellow co-workers. My mind was a complete chatter box; I lived in the past and the future all the time.

I didn't understand the present at all, I continually let it pass me by, as I strayed from one topic to the next inside my head. I remember making concerted efforts looking at clouds, and the color of the sky, trying to focus on one item at a time. Eventually I was getting better at noticing my present moment and the colors and textures around me, but my mind still bounced around like Tigger from *Winnie the Pooh*.

I knew I had a lot of work to do if I was going to succeed at being more present, more confident, and eliminating the chatter in my head, but it was important in order to make an impact in my current work environment. I needed to find and bring my best self forward in order to create a stronger sense of purpose at this studio, and I needed some spiritual guidance to infiltrate my soul and infuse my work with a different sort of passion. This was my first step toward the light and understanding the importance of being.

The months were fleeing by, and Toy Fair was fast approaching. This industry tradeshow was one of the biggest, where all the new toys were being showcased years in advance. Hasbro,

Mattel, and all the toy giants had showrooms that were several stories high with hired actors and actresses selling their future toy lines with scripted performances, sizzle videos, and on-air commercials as their show reels.

Toy Fair was one of those prestigious shows where invites to parties and glances at Mattel's showroom were hard tickets to get, and if you got one, you were part of the "in" crowd. Almost everyone at SPCP was able to get the hard invites, so I always managed to enjoy the privilege of working at the studio with the perks that came along with it.

At this particular Toy Fair, SPCP needed to launch *Godzilla The Movie,* and it needed to be as monumental as the creature itself. Peter worked closely with Roland Emmerich and Dean Devlin, the Director and Producer of the movie, to obtain teaser footage that he could use to sell licenses worldwide. A licensing launch is always eighteen months prior to film release, and *Godzilla* had special restrictions, including not being able to show the creature until the actual movie premiere. We all worked closely with the production team, and it was an honor and privilege to be among such great talent.

I never took the perks of this business for granted, nor did I allow myself to feel I was better than anyone else. My experience at Saban was a humbling one, as one minute you are accepting an award, and the next minute you are packing up your office and being escorted out by human resources.

Saban taught me a very important lesson: I learned there is no permanent state of being, and Planet Earth is a vulnerable place where our futures change in a nanosecond. Even the Earth itself is unstable as the crust shifts and shakes, and volcanoes erupt to create new land masses. Nothing is permanent. I stayed focused and enjoyed the offerings and perks of the business but remained humble knowing that it could be taken away with a blink of an eye.

Toy Fair was held in Manhattan every February, and the weather was quite unpredictable. I flew to New York prior to the show to secure room blocks for our hotel stay and searched around the area to see where I could wrap an entire building with our Godzilla tag Line: "Size Does Matter." We wanted to own Toy Fair and wanted *Godzilla* to be the most requested license at the show, so I canvassed the Flat Iron Building as it was directly across the street from the Toy Building and would provide a great backdrop for our marketing campaign.

I returned from New York and hired a production company to provide me a Request for Quote (RFQ) for wrapping the building, which would include a lighting package and the costs of obtaining the appropriate permits. I went through several budget revisions with Peter, and we all decided that it would be better to have a dotted line of reporting to both the VP of Marketing and

Peter as we worked on a great deal of confidential material. The dotted line worked out well as Peter had a specific vision, and we needed to understand it and adhere to it clearly, in order to move forward. Being able to go to him directly, meant speeding up projects, minimizing deadlines, and implementing complicated scenarios quickly and efficiently.

The Toy Fair budget was approved, and the Flat Iron Building would be wrapped *Godzilla*-style for all the Toy Fair world to see, and we opted out of a launch party as we weren't allowed to show the creature. An eye and a leg were all that we were able to show the licensing community and the rest would lay on *Godzilla's* shoulders based on his history and television equity.

The Flat Iron Building was wrapped, our room block secured as key execs from the SPCP department ventured off to Toy Fair and got a glimpse of my work ethic for the first time. The executives were pleasantly surprised, and the President of Worldwide Marketing applauded Peter's efforts as we monopolized Toy Fair. *Godzilla* was the buzz of the show, and my reputation within the department and licensing community began to grow. My anxiety level diminished a bit as I continued to produce high level productions and events for the entire division.

I also produced events for the retail division and eased into relationships with many of the executives at SPCP, but Juli was one of my favorites. She was Head of Retail. She was sharp witted, cunning, intelligent, creative, and had a big personality. Juli had the largest blue eyes I had ever seen, and this soft southern drawl that made her that much more charming.

She used to walk around the office and occasionally tell everyone she was in a "mood deluxe," secretly meaning something had ruffled her feathers or an urgent fire burst forth and she needed to put on her retail hat and extinguish it immediately. Sometimes she would need teams of people to come together on her behalf, and we were always happy to do so. Retail was a key division because without retail space you had no products to sell.

I began to see some similarities between Saban and Sony, as some team members banded together to save others, but there were still a few that were more than happy to throw you under the bus and call it a day. I never saw a drop of sweat off Juli's face nor a semblance of wavering in her eyes as she was always in control, always knew how to handle the most difficult situations with grace. I learned many things from Juli, one of the more poignant being, "don't let them see you sweat." I didn't have much of a poker face, and Juli was a master. Watching her in action was much like a magic show, as she grabbed your attention and captivated you to believe and buy whatever she was selling.

Juli needed my office to create a retail road-show to feature our upcoming properties so the retailers could prepare in advance and allot us shelf space for our future products. Planograms for shelf space were prepared months in advance of product release, and if we weren't on those planograms, then we didn't get shelf space. It was an extremely competitive market, and Juli was a persuasive talker. She not only wanted shelf space, but she wanted to secure feature areas within Walmart, Target, and Kmart stores, as mass market was the moneymaker, and we needed to be part of the revenue flow.

Juli was a beautiful spirit and a swaying storyteller, and she would come down to my office frequently to give me advice about how to handle an executive or how to remain graceful and poised during a stressful situation. Her stories and life journey encapsulated me for hours outside of Sony, and I grew to love her. She inspired my soul, my direction, my inner voice, and had wisdom far beyond her years. She only knew how to win, and she didn't do it at other's expense.

She was gracious and kind, and very much a female version of Peter. I was blessed to be in the presence of two inspiring souls who spoke with actions, and led with integrity, kindness, and humility. I didn't know it, but at the time I was being embossed with a positive and inspiring imprint that would stay with me for an entire lifetime and being present would continue to play a larger role as I checked in for longer periods of time.

Several weeks after Toy Fair wrapped, I was about to get a new officemate, or at least someone right next door to me. She would be the Creative Director of SPCP, and her name was Christiane. She was European born, raised in Germany, and was a bright light from day one, and I couldn't figure out how lucky I was to be around such luminous spirits, but then again, nothing is coincidence.

She moved in, introduced herself, and we became true friends. She understood the world like no other, and I was to grow fifty times faster because Christiane's office was next door to mine. We shared everything together. She taught me about print and the four-color process, CYMK (Cyan, Yellow, Magenta and Black). She allowed me to see deeply into her world, and I let her deeply into mine. We were like brother and sister, connected by the hip, and if Christiane was in a meeting, then most likely I would be there too.

Peter understood our connection, and he thought it was amusing that we went everywhere together. We worked closely on many projects, and she introduced me to the art world and her flavorful friends in the art community.

I learned style guide creation, including patterns and borders, and her creative process. She hired talented freelancers, such as Alissa Effland, and I would visit the freelance room throughout my day just to get inspiration and connect with the creatives. I didn't consider myself a creative at the time, but that would soon change as I evolved and understood myself better.

The *Godzilla* movie release was upon us, and Peter wanted my office to produce a movie premiere, a party that everyone would attend including the president of the studio. Theatrical marketing was producing a premiere in the streets of New York, so I thought I would do the opposite and go way up high and utilize a penthouse and show off the scale of *Godzilla* through a luxury space above the clouds.

I canvassed penthouse spaces in Manhattan prior to the movie release, and visited numerous premiere worthy locations including Windows of the World on the 106th floor of what used to be part of the twin towers prior to 9/11. I opted for a boutique penthouse space on the Upper East Side, which sported a three-hundred and sixty degree wrap of Manhattan.

Luckily my event direction would prove successful as the majority of studio executives preferred sitting in the VIP area of a penthouse sipping champagne and enjoying appetizers that would satiate even the most difficult palette. I recall being on headset at the premiere party escorting VIPs to their appropriate areas and greeting them upon arrival in my black pin striped suit and Armani tie that I could barely afford at the time. An open bar provided some fun and adventure as executives loosened up and celebrated the success of the movie release.

The penthouse decision was a solid one, as the head of the studio stopped by for an aperitif. Peter gained departmental recognition, which was important in an industry that was so incestuous. There was a little part of me that wondered if my luck would run out or if something lived deep inside me that drove me to create the proper scenarios.

I needed to explore this further and dive into some serious soul searching to understand my character and abilities at a deeper level. In 2001 I would take that dive, but for now I would stay safe under the studio umbrella alongside my protectorates as I moved forward to make the studio as much licensing money as I could, building a strong marketing services and event program.

Well, *Godzilla* was released, and the box office numbers were lackluster and far below the projections from the distribution execs. We were all working on so many different projects, as there were so many intellectual properties which stole our focus that we literally just moved on, accepted it, and tried to surpass it with something new on the horizon. The *Spider-Man* franchise was that something new, and what a web-bouncing ride Spidey would be, as we were in the same position with CGI footage and hiding Spidey's new armor and outfit prior to the movie release.

Remember that we launched eighteen months prior to film release, so gathering assets was a challenge, as we couldn't go directly to the studio, and many times we had to go directly to production. Christiane and I were selected to go to Marvel's headquarters in New York and look at their archives to gather creative assets and information for the style guide, the tradeshow launch, as well as the theatrical press event. I have to say it was such an honor to have access to such privileged artwork, and we were both excited to see what we could learn about our friendly neighborhood *Spider-Man.*

We arrived in New York, and it was quite warm for March, as we strolled through the streets and prepared for our meeting in the morning. Anyone who is familiar with Manhattan weather will tell you that it can easily be seventy degrees one moment, and within two hours, might completely change and drop thirty degrees.

We woke up in the morning to snow and a city covered in white. Neither Christiane nor I brought winter clothes during March, so we decided to make the most out of our light California attire, and we would just hail taxis and avoid the outside as much as possible. Apparently, taxis don't operate in the city during a snowstorm, and most of the shops were closed, so we gathered up our frozen bodies and tried to get cozy with the subway system as it was our only means to get us to Marvel.

We arrived ten minutes late, but few seemed to notice as the door swung open past security, and we were greeted by two upper-level executives who escorted us down a long, narrow hallway and into the Marvel archives. This room hosted original art that dated back to the inception of Marvel and the creation of the first Marvel comic book. It was difficult to comprehend the vast history that sat in this room, and for a few hours, it was all ours as we asked questions and viewed original artwork from Stan Lee.

Spidey's character positions were all trademarked as there were style guide poses that would need to appear on packaging, patterns and borders, and all licensed products that showcased his face and likeness. He was a complex character whose armor and likeness changed through his years of comic evolution. We learned so much about our little neighborhood *Spider-Man* that day, the intricacies of his life, his personality, and his special abilities.

Our New York trip was a quick turnaround, and we jetted back to Los Angeles promptly, excited to share our newfound facts about our friend Spidey. Upon returning, Peter met with both of us in the morning, looking inquisitive, as his furrowed brow deepened and his voice became quite serious; he explained that we may have jeopardized our relationship with Marvel. Christiane and I were dumbfounded. We each tried to formulate the appropriate words to assist Peter in working out this sordid misunderstanding. Working at any job can be political but working in entertainment had a political undertow that could throw even the most accomplished swimmer out to sea.

Firings at Sony Pictures were frequent as we were all privy to screaming executives being carried down the hallway by security guards, while their things were being packed and shipped to the Producer's Building, as they were no longer allowed on the lot.

After discussing our Marvel meeting with Peter, we came to the conclusion that it was my inability to eat the white-breaded sandwiches that Marvel supplied at lunch that upset them. I do try and eat healthy, and I don't eat bread. Based on my lack of bread eating capabilities, our relationship with Marvel went a little sideways for the time being but would be salvaged in a day or two after they forgot about the sandwiches and focused on Spidey. Christiane and I always laughed about that moment, and calling ourselves the sacrificial lambs, occasionally making lambs sounds as we laughed about the business we were in and how superficial it could be at times.

Spidey's momentum was growing as we prepared for the upcoming MAGIC Apparel Show in Vegas, which would entice all the new apparel buyers, and SPCP had a huge presence on the show floor showcasing our upcoming properties and highlighting our friendly neighborhood *Spider-Man*. Spidey was going to debut as a live action character for his first time, intermingled with state of the art CGI, as he swung into the streets of Manhattan. During setup, I remember receiving a phone call at our tradeshow booth in Vegas; to my surprise it was my father.

To give you a little background, my biological father and I couldn't really see much of each other when I was growing up, as my mom forbade me to see him. They divorced when I was five years old. It was quite a strain on our relationship, and when I did see him, it was always sad to return home to the chaos and uncertainty.

He would send me cards, but my mom would intercept them, toss them in the trash and I would come to find out years later from conversations with my Father that he never missed a Birthday or special holiday without thinking of his son.

When I was eighteen, and legally more in control of my life, I started getting closer to my dad and started building a solid relationship with him. Sadly, we didn't have much time together, or so I would soon find out as he began explaining to me that his body was tired of dialyzing, the bone cancer from dialysis was progressing and now was the time I needed to see him and say goodbye.

As previously explained during my time at Special Services, my dad was one hundred percent disabled from the service. While in the service he contracted the strep virus, the nurses pumped antibiotics too quickly into his system, and the strep virus moved to his kidneys and literally ate them. He started dialysis at a very young age, and by the time I received this phone call, my dad was only sixty.

He had exhausted every last vein in his body trying to plug in to dialyze and his body was slowly shutting down.

My dad was tired and ready to leave the planet and this phone call was his way of saying goodbye. I hung up the phone, blankly, staring off into space, my lifeline suddenly disconnected from the planet.

I was left floating in space for several moments without a sound or thought in my head. My breath and heart beat quieted, the silence enveloped my entire being and I floated further and further away. It was one of the quietest moments I can remember, filled with an inexplicable sadness that was impossible to digest.

I was suddenly interrupted, jarred back to Earth by a co-worker who was concerned about my languid movements and frozen persona. At that moment I informed everyone at the booth that my dad was passing away, and I needed to leave things at the booth dangling for now to be present for my Father as he left this Earth, shed his body shell, and let his spirit take flight.

I asked everyone to work together as a team and get us through MAGIC. Many of them began shoving cash in my pocket, telling me that I was going to need it, and to just take it and worry about repayment later.

Peter arranged for my flight and rental car, and before I knew it, I was in Menlo Park, California, confused and sad at the prospect of never seeing my father again. It was a long process, but the morphine drip provided some comfort as the process of departing took several days. I could intuitively tell that he was struggling a bit, and leaned my head down beside his ear, to whisper words of comfort, letting him know that I was going to make him proud and being a man meant that I could hold my own now, and he needn't worry.

I laid my head on his chest and it was this moment that he decided to pass his spirit through mine and leave his body shell behind for good. I spent the next few days organizing the funeral and his memorial. I dressed him in an Armani Suit. He was Italian, and he liked those nice suits that fit snug on the body and accentuated all the right places. He was an artist and studied Tai Chi and would occasionally take me to classes where I would see him focused on one leg moving slowly through the meditative artform.

My father was a spiritual being and would tell me stories about his mother performing seances and tables floating and spirits visiting the room. It was all too farfetched for me to understand in the moment, but I loved his stories and his passion for life. He was married seven times, and he used to tell me that life was a banquet and we needed to taste it fully. He tried every color of the rainbow, and sometimes he would repeat the colors simply because he ran out of PMS color options.

I learned a lot about death, as it was my first time visiting this closely and looking into its eyes head on. I wasn't finely tuned and in touch with my mortality and that I too would turn to dust one day, but at that moment it woke me up and jarred me violently. Death parades around with a solemn stance, but it too has hidden agendas, much like the world of the living. Promises that were stated while he was alive, would soon diminish from others as he passed into another dimension.

I was disgusted with the lack of integrity as others tried to grab property, money, and decide who would be the rightful heir to his estate. He had no will to pass on, so it became quite ugly. I didn't care about the money. I just wanted more time with my father, and that wasn't going to happen. I always thought death would be this honorable moment where people come together and finally let go of the past, but it's not. It can be darker and even uglier than I could have ever imagined.

I flew back to Los Angles, and took a few days for myself. I arrived inside my apartment and slid down the wall right outside my door. I had no energy, and I sat there lifeless, trying to digest the last week or so, my hands cupping my head in disbelief as I slowly plotted my next course of action. I knew that getting back to work would occupy my mind, so I phoned Peter and told him I would be returning to work in the morning.

Shortly after returning to the studio, 9/11 became the national news and the country stood still as we watched it invaded by terrorists. The movie industry stopped, as did many industries, and we all suddenly found ourselves laid off and unemployed.

CHAPTER 4

Discovery

I lay awake in a dormant cocoon
Wrapped in a vessel of stranded perfection
Waiting listlessly for my sprouted wings
And my streamline corpus to emerge
With the quiet mind I sleep in silence
It is patience's path that guides me thus
Into the morrow and dawn of a new day

Still grieving from the death of my father, and now being jobless, gave me absolute permission to hide under a rock and not come out for a very long time. I did just that and hid from view. I call it cocooning, where you hide inside a cocoon, and when you're ready, you break open the chrysalis and emerge as a beautiful butterfly. I cocooned for approximately two years of my life and decided to take up oil painting to honor my father. I didn't take classes but just touched the brush on the canvas, and knew I had found something deeply meaningful, feeling the brush softly hit the lightly textured white linen square. The chatter in mind was silenced. I would go an entire day without eating or going to the bathroom as I was unaware of time passing.

The day would turn to night as the light would dim outside my kitchen window, and suddenly I would be aware that my feet hurt from standing all day, yet while painting, I felt no pain. Painting would become my best friend, my lover, and everything else in between. I would be complete, needing or wanting nothing as I continued my journey filling up as many canvases as I could, with Modigliani-type portraits of women from the Renaissance. I'm not sure where they came from exactly, but I knew that I was connected to this art form and I couldn't stop painting these mysterious women that belonged in some kind of time-traveled dimension of their own.

Time was slipping by, and my finances were slowly diminishing. I would apply for jobs in entertainment, but there was no movement at all. It's as if the job market just stood still, and we were all staring at each other in disbelief. I was an avid antique collector at the time and decided to start selling items on eBay. eBay's reputation was growing, and many trusted the platform and relied on it to supplement their income. It was simply a matter of survival and the first items sold were the higher-priced items: jewelry, gold, and designer silver. As my unemployment stint progressed into a long-term lag, there was nothing I wouldn't sell, and the venetian mirrors and oil paintings on the walls became scarce. My one-bedroom apartment should have sported a vacancy sign outside, as one piece after another became liquidated either through consignment or online sales. I learned via the entertainment world to show others your success and wealth by wearing jewelry and fancy designer labels. Unemployment taught me to lose my attachment to objects and material things and find your inner peace and joy through quiet expression and creativity.

Quite honestly, I experienced a great deal of joy being unemployed, and I think I really needed a break from my hellacious event schedule at the studio. I was still grieving, and I savored being alone. I think many of us fear being alone, and we look at its confinement as something negative as the world tells us to connect and find someone meaningful so that we can be complete and joyful. I found my joy for those two years, hidden away in my sweet cocoon where the chatter of my mind was mitigated through a meditative state I would later describe as my creative state of being. All those years, I obsessed over material objects that I placed in my home to validate myself and impress others. The objects were a façade of deceit, and a cacophony of clutter, as they made their way to other happy homes across the nation.

I continued applying for jobs, as there were fewer objects to sell, and very little to liquidate in order to cover my rent. I wasn't depressed or scared about the prospect of what I would become, as I had my faith in God, and I knew I would survive this. I wasn't completely aware of my evolution in life, but I completely understood that being unemployed changed my focus and created a stronger alignment with my soul. I felt I had a better grasp on the importance of being whole and what that meant.

I had no connection with objects or material things other than the paintings that were born every time I would create. These paintings were the core of my existence, and the joy they gave me was inexplicable, each creation was like giving birth to a new child, a child that would live forever on a plane that I would not. The bond between my father and I would live on as long as I held a brush in my hand and swept it across a canvas. Unemployment taught me to find joy and happiness deep within myself, during a time of solitude. It's those little awakenings in the darkest caverns of the abyss that surprise me the most. Incredible growth appears when we least expect it, so I stopped searching for it and simply allowed it to arrive.

After being unemployed for approximately two years, I finally received a call from a company in Carlsbad, California, as they were looking for an Events Manager. Carlsbad was just a snippet outside of San Diego, and about three hours from Los Angeles. I wasn't sure I was ready to leave LA, but I didn't have the luxury of waiting for the right opportunity to fly through my painting window and smack me in the face, so I embraced this new journey with fortitude. The Upper Deck Company (UDC) required several interviews, and each interview would mean a three-hour drive each way. The UDC had two divisions: an entertainment division and a sports division. I was well versed in entertainment, but I truly knew little about the sports world, and I wasn't sure if I would be a strong fit for the position. Perhaps because of working in entertainment, I was flashier than most, and I could envision some of the sports guys having a hard time with my "creative side."

During my final interview one of the sports guys asked me why I would want to move to Carlsbad after working for a major motion picture studio. He looked skeptical and wanted to know why I would take a downgraded position when I had so much experience. I told him the truth about the industry, and about 9/11, and that I wanted to continue making an impact producing events and felt I could do that at Upper Deck. Several weeks later I received the job offer from UDC, and I had two weeks to move as the offer had a moving bonus, and they needed me to start as soon as possible. I couldn't figure out the sense of urgency, but I needed the work, and the sooner I received a paycheck, the better.

I hopped in my car and waved goodbye to Los Angeles as the palm trees swayed in the wind and the smog hung over the city like a poorly ventilated cigar bar. I would miss the studio and the friendships I nurtured, and the entertainment tingle I would get when a new project was greenlit. For now, I was bound further south, but I hoped to return someday and would wait patiently for a resurgence after 9/11, as I hopped in my car and drove to La Jolla, California. I could have moved to Carlsbad, but I really wanted to be closer to the city and the ocean. UDC was headquartered in Carlsbad, and was about thirty minutes outside of La Jolla, and it would have been even further had I moved to downtown San Diego. I was right in between the two, and I felt a balance and symmetry with my decision.

La Jolla spawned magical scenery right out of a picture book. The cove was drenched by boutique restaurants and art galleries, and my gym was directly across the street from the charm of the city. The gym happened to be attached to the La Jolla Hilton, so all of the amenities of the hotel flowed into the pool area as one was able to get poolside service at the snap of a finger after finishing a workout. This was one of the many perks of joining a gym of this stature, but I was cautious and careful about dipping into the material world once again, so I slowly enjoyed the perks from an objective point of view. I had a better perspective of that world, and its powerful, luring capabilities.

The following morning I arrived at Upper Deck, reported to Human Resources, and was given a tour. I supplied them with my moving receipts, which washed away any moving bonus they provided. I assumed Upper Deck was a small company, and I would be a big fish in a small pond coming from Sony Pictures Entertainment. I was certainly wrong about my assessment, as the company was extremely large and spanned over several floors. The lobby was impressive, and the entry way was garnished with small ponds and plants that stretched toward the sun. It was a massive compound, which operated out of a building owned by the CEO Richard McWilliam. I was shown to my cubicle, which was directly below a skylight and perched in the middle of a room surrounded by eight other cubicles. I had a couple of bouts of skin cancer a few years prior, and I wasn't so keen on sitting under a skylight, nor was I going to be happy that I would have to wear sunscreen to work. I was a bit surprised that I didn't have an office, but I certainly didn't want to start my job requiring certain things and garnering a reputation for being high maintenance. The skylight through me off, and so did the cubicle, but so did being unemployed for the last two years, so I took a stance of gratefulness and worked below a skylight for the following six months.

Later that day I was introduced to some of the executives in both the sports and entertainment divisions and immediately felt tension from the sports guys, but the entertainment folks embraced my can-do attitude with vigor. Perhaps it was my energy and thought process, but I intuitively knew I had some hurdles to traverse if I were going to be successful in my new position. All of this sounded so familiar to me much like a broken record that kept skipping over the same groove as the word Saban stranded itself inside my endless mind chatter for an eternity.

HR confirmed my instinctual apprehension as they also warned me that I would need to make some changes in the department and that it might be a bit bumpy the first few months. I received another warning from the VP of Marketing, as she was my direct report. Prior to Upper Deck she worked at Mattel, so we had a strong connection, and understood the toy world well.

She also struggled in Los Angeles finding work and found herself in the same position searching outside the city for opportunities. She warned me that this environment was unique, and I would need to tread cautiously as it wasn't the entertainment world that I was used to. I was confused by her statement, but I received two warnings the same day, and would get a third later that day from a coworker. I forgot about the corporate world and the politics of it all, and unbeknownst to me I was about to be thrown into the ring of fire with no armor or weapons to be found.

I attended my first few meetings the following morning and watched as the Athlete Relations team formalized their details for the upcoming Tiger Woods event and pretended that I wasn't in the room. It certainly wasn't the kindest or warmest welcome. I asked to see the budget and kindly let them know that I would be handling the details and creative side for the event, and they simply laughed, saying, "Sure, whatever." I guess my thoughts on designing topiary for the golf course in the shape UD logo would have to wait as Upper Deck traditionally flew banners and posters outside to make a statement. I also wanted to tie off logos on all the water holes and use fishing line to secure them so the company logo would be floating in the middle of each hole. I had some fun ideas, but I was forced to table them until the next meeting or many meetings thereafter.

Some meetings would start without me, or I wouldn't get an invite at all, and I wasn't going to tolerate much more of the peculiar antics. I made some assessments with my current team and reported back to HR with replacement suggestions. They supported my decision, and I ended up hiring someone new for the department and aligning myself with one other team member whose background was vast, including working for the Olympic Games.

He was an experienced event planner, highly detailed, and as much as he thought it strange to have a new boss from the film world, we became great friends. Tim was my first real alliance at Upper Deck, and there was nothing we couldn't accomplish together as he was an avid sports enthusiast and knew all the players in every sport imaginable. I was not as well versed in the sports world, and Tim bridged the gap with the sports guys, when he embraced me, so did a few others inside the company.

Tim challenged me with questions and processes, and he brought out my best self. I was grateful to be working alongside such a gifted soul. We were truly the Dynamic Duo. Things were starting to come together, but it would be a slow and arduous journey to get everyone on board with the new event style, design, and schedule.

I focused on staying present and tried not to listen to all the chatter that surrounded my cube. It was a noisy hub of personalities, and one easily lost focus by engaging in the chatter. I had a lot of work to do, and I couldn't afford to be distracted by the noise. A few tenured employees were surprised that I had already hired someone new, and they were skeptical with my agenda and plans for the company's event future.

As for the rest of the company, I would let my work speak for itself, stay positive, and focus on raising the stature of the brand. I had two hundred and forty events to produce each year, and I would have plenty of opportunity to prove my team's capabilities and let our creativity shine. The Vice President of Marketing's advice was wise, as it was a tough environment and I wasn't a traditional sports guy so I would rely on a few creative miracles to persuade the sports team to root me on.

Inside the entertainment division, it was a completely different story. A vast majority of this team were hard core gamers, and they loved outside-the-box thinking and savory creative choices that would make them stand out. They welcomed me on my first day, were respectful in meetings, and were extremely engaging. I did have some game background, and I played Dungeons and Dragons in school, and they all thought that was extremely cool. The Sports Division thought I was the outcast or black sheep of the "boys club" while the Entertainment Division thought I was the "cool guy."

It's interesting how the world tags us into categories, without seeking our core truth and essence of being, and we work so hard to shatter their false image of us, while craving some form of validation and acceptance. I'm tired of being a brand on a shelf which gets shipped off to the discount stores because the decision makers no longer believe in the strength or power of the brand.

Why is it so difficult to give someone a chance to succeed or an opportunity to prove their worth and why must we continually bleed for our supper? We work so hard to dissuade others when they have already selected the outcome without opening their mind to our real selves.

We simply want to be accepted for who we are, without having to conform or perform some ritual or rite which inevitably grates against us like sandpaper, much like a tawdry piece of wood that withers into dust from over sanding. At the end of the story, we're not a piece of wood anymore at all, but some fragmented piece of dust that the world designed as we forget about our real selves and slip into a conformed reality in order to survive. I wasn't going to be beaten by the sport team's bullying, and I think that's what saved me from becoming another piece of dust on their shelf. I was a challenge for them, and with my utmost fortitude, I was bound to persevere without losing my soul in the process.

Later that month, the Vice President of Marketing called me in her office to have a heartfelt chat about my performance. She felt that my position wasn't working out and that it would be best for me to probably seek other employment. I was saddened by what I was hearing and retaliated with scenarios that had transpired the last month, which she understood.

She told me that she was fearful this would happen, and she knew the entertainment division would embrace me, and it would be more challenging with the sports division. She started to give me some tips on how to navigate through the shark tank, and she gave me two more weeks to turn things around. That meant dropping the ego and coming from a place of humility, and not being upset when meetings would start without me.

I was extremely rusty after living in my own cocoon for two years, and completely forgot about the intricacies of the workplace. At Sony, ego was looked upon as a form of survival, where at Upper Deck it had the opposite effect; it would quickly be my demise. Meetings ran smoother, and I waited patiently for my turn to speak. I was conscious of not overwhelming the team with my creative ideas, and I tiptoed around, listening more, and speaking less. At the close of the meetings I would recap some of the highlights, and the different teams became used to my style and demeanor. Things did turn around, and I was to learn a great deal about myself, and how to manage a successful team as we all lunged forward towards the finish line.

Months later we moved to different floors and all the managers got offices, which meant I could leave my beloved skylight and pack up my sunscreen for a summer day rather than a jaunt to the office. My space was next door to the Manager of Advertising, and she would play a critical role in helping me achieve some further alignment with the sports division.

Her name was Kristy Watson, and we spent countless hours together discussing the dynamics of Upper Deck. She helped me navigate, I helped her with creativity, and together we built a solid friendship. Much like my officemate at Sony, Kristy was an authentic soul, and we shared everything together, including half-priced wine nights on Wednesdays in the heart of Del Mar. One day in the hallway she shared something with me that was a bit more disconcerting, and I did my best to simply listen, as speaking less and listening more seemed to be a winning combination.

She backed me up into a wall as she spoke softly, almost whispering so others wouldn't hear: "Don't disappoint me, Greg. I voted for you, and I am the reason you got this job. You are not at Sony, and this is not a glamorous place, so you need to tone it down, and just do the simple things that can move us all forward." I was uncertain why this topic was so passionately spouting from her lips, but she was obviously triggered about a scenario or perhaps a rumor from another coworker. I didn't say much that day, but inside I did feel Upper Deck was glamorous, and I wanted this company to be the envy of the world. It had tremendous potential, and glamour was a part of its future. That world lived inside my soul, and I couldn't just stuff it away and ignore my eternal calling.

Later that same month Tim and I produced a celebrity filled Super Bowl party in Houston, and in tow with my event background, it was only appropriate to roll out the red carpet and step-and-repeat logos, which would provide the perfect backdrop for celebrity photo ops. Rain was predicted the eve of the celebrity gathering, so I hired fifty temps to hang outside the logoed railing and assist on drawing a crowd as four hundred models swayed up the red carpet single file and disappeared beneath the UDC awning. The gathering outside the railing grew as celebrities began to arrive, including Peyton Manning who stood in front of the step-and-repeat logoed wall while several photographers captured his essence through their professional lenses. The rain never arrived, and the crowd grew massive as the CEO of UDC arrived with an entourage of more celebrities and executives from the company as they stepped out of their black stretch limousines.

Richard looked startled and a bit confused as he sauntered up the red carpet amassing the size and scope of the crowd behind the railing and the pulse of the night ahead. As I maneuvered through the party, I noticed Kristy sipping champagne at the bar surrounded by sports celebrities and key executives from UDC. I walked up behind her and whispered softly in her ear, "is it me or do you look extremely glamorous at this extremely glamorous affair or perhaps you'd like to describe your feeling in your own words?" as I smiled with a large Cheshire-cat grin. She put down her glass of champagne, stood up from her chair, and gave me the warmest hug, as her arms clung tight around my shoulders. She was about to speak, and I slowly pressed my index finger against her lips, telling her, silently, that we both understood her answer. The party continued into the wee hours of the morning, and we all slunk onto a plane shortly afterward, returning home to Carlsbad, California.

The Sports Division's attitude shifted after the Super Bowl party, and the Athlete Relations team would swing by my office to shoot the breeze and reminisce about their special party highlights as they laughed, patted me on the back, and looked forward to the next one.

I graciously said, "thank you," and reminded them to go outside and thank Tim for his hard work. Speaking of thanking Tim, I received two tickets, while in Houston, to the big Super Bowl game after our industry party, and I gave them to Tim as a thank you. This was a bucket list item for him, and he could now cross off that he attended Super Bowl XXXVIII. He poured his soul into his work, and we *spilled blood* together to make the insurmountable happen time and again. The company was proud of our achievements, and I was slowly feeling more comfortable at Upper Deck. It started to feel more like a family than a workplace. I think I found a new home outside of LA, and it started to feel warm, pleasant, and more than cozy.

The day ended with an unexpected visit from the CEO, as he was rumored to be downstairs, and this was an anomaly as we always went up to the "C" Level if we were summoned by him or had a question that we would pose to his Assistant. This was an unusual scenario, I could hear him asking where Gregory Copploe sat, and others directed him to my office. He popped his face in my doorway, entered my office and closed the door. I could feel the energy of the entire company looming outside as he sat down and threw the cover of the *USA Today* paper on my desk. Richard explained that he disliked the step-and-repeat wall at the party and felt it was ugly and distasteful, but he understood its intent, as I looked at the cover and saw Peyton Manning standing in front of our UDC logo, repeated behind him.

Richard had never received this kind of free publicity at a gathering that his event department had thrown, and he left a mysterious envelope on my desk and thanked me again for our Super Bowl accomplishments as he departed. The envelope contained an obscene amount of money, and I called Tim inside my office to split the proceeds with him as other employees came running in to glance at the *USA Today* cover and ask questions about Richard's visit to the basement. I think I had finally left my imprint at Upper Deck, and whatever issues I had in the past would melt away and be forgotten as Greg was now officially "cool" with both divisions.

I spent three years of my life at Upper Deck and practically lived on airplanes most of the time. The schedule was grueling, and my team and I rarely got a break as the pace was much faster than at Sony Pictures. As far as the glamour goes, it was alive and well as the CEO would cancel my commercial flights many times, and his limo would pick me up and drop me off at his Gulfstream IV, on which we would all fly privately.

I had never flown privately while at Sony, so this was a new addition to my life that I thoroughly enjoyed, and it ended up ruining any chance of enjoying a regular commercial flight in the future. I was spoiled and never imagined that this trading card company would show me a world that was very similar or better to the one I lived in Los Angeles. The dichotomy of life was interesting indeed. One moment I would be eating tuna sandwiches, painting in my apartment, unemployed, watching every penny, and the next moment I am eating baby rack of lamb inside a Gulfstream IV and sipping on a glass of Opus One while attending a Tiger Woods Golf Clinic at the Grand Cypress Golf Resort in Orlando, Florida. It was a whirlwind of change, and I didn't understand how life could be so dramatically different and dangle me at two completely opposite ends of the spectrum. There was a lesson in all of this, and I was about to learn it.

My office neighbor, Kristy, introduced me to one of her vendors shortly after we wrapped the Tiger Woods Clinic. Kristy felt that I would have a strong connection with her as she was spiritual in nature and had a similar alignment. I arranged a lunch meeting with Sharon at a little waterfront restaurant in Encinitas, hoping to connect with her and just have a casual conversation about life and its purpose.

I was searching for answers and couldn't fathom being unemployed months earlier and then suddenly flying on private planes all over the U.S. The planet seemed so unstable, and I felt like I was being tossed around like a buoy on a vociferous sea, and I simply wanted a bit more control with the outcome. Sharon was already seated, and she summoned me over to our table with a soft wave of her hand. I told her I would be wearing a baseball cap, so she must have known it was me when I arrived. She had big brown eyes that were inquisitive and burned through my soul.

Sharon would share with me later that I had the same deep-seated look. We got through the basic formalities and then dove right into the core subjects that were challenging both of us. I asked her why she left Upper Deck, and she spoke about toxicity and being around toxic people and that the environment wasn't aligned with her spirit. She wanted to build something meaningful and felt that she couldn't complete that task at Upper Deck. She started her own Public Relations Firm and began consulting with several organizations around the country.

I wanted to know more about toxicity because I felt some toxic energy in my life through friendships, relationships, and my work environment, and I wanted to understand the term a bit better and how one manages the leap from toxic to oxygenated freedom. Sharon had some great answers as she took me through some of her journey as she explained the following: "Toxicity arrives in our lives at some point, and the first break up point of departing from its grasp is acknowledging that it's there. We must be awake and be present to discover its presence and allow ourselves to feel deeply, even if it means being uncomfortable. The biggest power toxicity has over us is our inability to leave a toxic situation due to fear. We handcuff ourselves because we are afraid of being alone or leaving a work situation and being unemployed. Many live most of their lives in fear, and few actually break free from it to have a fuller existence on the planet."

My brain remained in a porous, sponge-like state, absorbing as much information as I could. I was tired of being imprisoned by my own chatter, and I wanted to have a bit more control avoiding toxic people and toxic situations. Sharon replied, "Now, I can tell you that your energy is all over the place, and you need to hone in on it a bit. Our energy is better used when we specifically direct its intention towards something that can digest it". I didn't understand any of that conversation regarding my energy except that I gave too much away, and I agreed.

I picked up the check, but before I left, Sharon asked me to check out the teachings of *The Course of Miracles,* and that Marianne Williamson wrote a couple of books based on these teachings. She suggested that I might enjoy them and would feel a dramatic shift in my life by absorbing the spiritual content.

The teachings focused on love and minimizing fear and toxicity. I hugged Sharon goodbye, and returned to the office with a skip in my step, visualizing a hopeful future with less fear and attracting more love by simply being more loving.

I thanked Kristy for the introduction and gave her a little recap about our lunch meeting. My new thoughts and ideas would form a new direction and journey for my life, as I moved forward to fulfill my higher purpose and reduce the toxicity.

More than likely my circle of friends would become smaller, but I wasn't fearful of losing others but rather grateful to invite in a more uplifting and loving energy.

Interestingly, I tried to explain *The Course of Miracles* to others but few understood the concept, and I found myself wasting my energy trying to include others in my personal journey. I was so excited about it, and I wanted to share it with the world. I finally understood what Sharon meant about my energy that day when I met her at the restaurant and she explained that it was "all over the place". She was making a statement that you can't save the world, nor can you take everyone with you on your journey, so be cautious and aware of your energy and who you bequeath it to.

I kept my energy in check and gave it only to those who understood it, and those who couldn't digest it, I cautiously held it back, and kept more energy for myself. Overall, I didn't feel as depleted. I was retaining more life energy simply by cautiously saving more energy for myself or spending my energy with those that could reciprocate by giving some in return.

Up until now I spent my life people pleasing, looking for validation from others, and being disappointed when I didn't receive it in return. It was time to fear less, experience more joy, and not wait for others to pat me on the back and validate me in some mysterious way as if it were important and gravely mattered. Validation comes from myself, and as long as I did my best, this should be all the validation I would ever need to complete my circle and inevitably feel more whole.

One thing spiritual people don't warn you about when you embark on a new journey is that you might discover you don't enjoy the life you are currently leading. Walking away is indeed an essential component of finding yourself and reducing your toxicity, but I wasn't sure I was ready to walk away. I could walk away from a few friendships, and I could walk away from a relationship because I had the power to manifest a better alignment with a new group of people, but I wasn't so certain in the job department.

Two years was a long time being unemployed, and it left a strong imprint of insecurity deep inside me. I was uncertain and still fearful of walking away. I kept telling myself I was happy, and I enjoyed my job, and for the most part I did, but I was burnt out. Three years of continually travelling away from my home, with my only friends being those that I worked with, meant I had no time to cultivate anything else meaningful. I lived on airplanes and inside hotel rooms across the country. I desired something more meaningful, and with that thought, change was on the horizon.

I completed another fifty or so events at Upper Deck including a Derek Jeter Clinic and LeBron James appearance. I enjoyed the appearances, but the tradeshows were sucking my life force away, and I couldn't deal with the redemption cards showing up late or a box missing on the show floor.

There were issues and obstacles at every show, and I was exhausted. I needed a plan, and I needed one quickly.

I asked Tim to step inside my office one day, and I shared with him the emptiness I was feeling in my current position. He was thankful for my honesty, and explained that he too was burnt out, and ready for a change. He wished the Olympic gigs were every year and would provide him with steady employment, as that was his dream job. Both Tim and I were burnt out, and I was to formulate a plan for our exit. Without fear on the backburner, I was able to dream bigger than before, and I wanted to run my own company and have Tim as my business partner.

Skybox Entertainment was born, and it was a delicious concept full of ripe opportunities in the event realm. Tim and I would run our own company hosting athlete events at prestigious skyboxes around the world, and guests would purchase a premium-priced ticket to hang with their favorite athletes. I created the Limited Liability Corporation and handled all the details, and Tim and I gave notice in July 2003 and departed Upper Deck. We were on our new journey creating athlete events, mixing both celebrities and fans together, to create bucket list moments for our die-hard fans.

A bit of bad luck fell our way as Hurricane Katrina would make landfall extremely close to our first athlete event appearance, and we had to cancel the entire event. I sunk all the money I had into this venture, and after paying off the athletes per their contract since we didn't have a force majeure clause, I was basically left with nothing, and the company dissolved. Tim went to work for Qualcomm, and I did the unemployment dance once again. I felt a bit dazed and confused, as I manifested this company and its direction, but failed to have the financial means to see it through. One thing I learned about manifesting is you need to be extremely specific about every detail. Failure wasn't something I imagined or manifested, nor was Hurricane Katrina, so I met with Sharon a second time to get additional clarity.

We met at the same place in Encinitas, and after describing my most recent adventures, she was pleased to see me growing. My energy wasn't haphazard and fragmented like it was during our initial meeting, and I kept plenty of energy for myself and for my personal rejuvenation.

She asked me if I was happy, and I said, "No." I was surprised as she laughed and smiled back at me with a twisted look on her face. "Greg, happiness isn't based on conditions. We aren't happy because something works out or something aligns with us. We are happy because we choose it in any situation. We are happy because we embrace it, and it lives within us. If we walked around waiting for the conditions to align so we could be happy, we would never reach that place of eternal happiness." It was a quick bite with

Sharon, but her words were dense and provided a deluge of wisdom and opportunity.

After leaving the restaurant, I decided that cocooning wouldn't be such a bad idea at this point as I just wanted to curl up and be alone. I was really exhausted from Upper Deck and starting Skybox, and I just needed a month or so to figure things out. I resided in my happy place, which was painting and spending a minimal amount of time with people. I found people exhausting, especially when I didn't have enough energy to give them, and I just wanted to experience a quiet mind.

Why wasn't I aware or willing to admit that painting was my happy place and not just a place I visited when I was cocooning? I think fear still lurked about and I couldn't quite connect the dots, but I was more aware of what painting provided and I knew that something powerful was growing inside of me. Meanwhile, I would be given an opportunity to relocate to Seattle, and I jumped at the chance of experiencing a new city and starting over. I was grateful that my unemployment was short lived.

One of my Upper Deck connections opened a gaming company in Seattle, and he wanted me to join the start up as Vice President of Marketing, Licensing, and Sales. I gasped at the title and laughed to myself wondering if it were possible for one individual to handle all three jobs, but I welcomed a new opportunity and a six-figure salary and jumped on a plane to Seattle. This story is a short one. I loved the people I worked with, but upper management was a distorted bag of confusion, and the CEO hired venture capitalists from LA to make the company more financially fit. The VCs had no vision or soul for the company, and it slowly dwindled away after seven short months. I found myself on the unemployment line again, and there was no time for cocooning. I was in a new city with zero connections, and I had no money in the bank and rent was due next month.

THE ART OF BEING WHOLE

CHAPTER 5

The Real Essence of Being

*Authentic to the touch as we slide our fingers
across the jutted surface
Painted chips flake forward like changing skins
that renew themselves
Masked in deception, our art of perception
We must peel back the layered tissue to view the
life beneath
The flowing river of plasma and mitochondria
Our visceral guise of vulnerability, raw and
unprotected
The Venetian mask slowly separated from its
sutures
And our core is left dancing naked for all to see*

I applied for jobs relentlessly, but Seattle was more of a tech city and favored those with computer science degrees who had a lust and passion for coding. I would have a few interviews, but no real connectivity, and was told by a Microsoft headhunter that I looked too Hollywood. I guess my inner nerd needed some guidance as I showed up in polished suits, freshly showered, and apparently this wasn't the typical scenario in Seattle. I stood out as a misfit once again. Dauntingly, the cycle continued as I was being buffed for the journey ahead. The interviews were sparse, which graciously allowed me more time to refine my artistic instrument as I found myself ready to exhibit and become vulnerable to the critique of the Seattle art scene.

I sent out a few jpegs to a few galleries while applying for "real" jobs, and a couple of them wrote back embracing my work and asking me to bring a few pieces down to the gallery in person. Warren Knapp Gallery in Capitol Hill was one of the first to honor my work and the liquidation of paintings brought in some solid side money while I was looking for my "real" job.

I state "real" job in quotes as its poignant that many of us who have a passion or drive for something on the side, rarely accept that this side job could actually be the "real" job in disguise. Does God send us messages that are fallen and undigested because we are unwilling to digest the truth, or are we easily beguiled into making inauthentic decisions based on the allurement of a particular position?

It's a curious thing this "looking for other jobs" as we do the self-talk chatter and explain that we need to apply for jobs that bring in a certain income regardless of alignment. I've had several jobs in my lifetime, but rarely admitted that my creative soul was that of an artist. Perhaps it was the fear from the old cliché, being a "starving artist" that kept me away, as I didn't do starving very well. One evening I had an *epiphany*, a monumental moment in time where truth reveals itself barreling down and puncturing the heart and soul; it revealed an enlightened and heightened vision of truth and awareness. The truth squeezed me emotionally and left me quiet as I sifted through its tranquil lucidity. At that moment I knelt to the floor, my legs swept underneath me forming the shape of cross, and I pressed my face and nose to the floor and spoke out loud:

"Dear God, I lie here scared and afraid to tell you my true thoughts and feelings. I know if I admit the truth, I will never be the same, and I know my life will dramatically change. It is this change that I am most fearful of as I enjoy money and the fruits that it brings, and I feel this truth that I'm about to bring you will solidify my destiny, and that scares me. I know in my heart that I am an artist. I am tired of pretending to be someone else. I simply want to live an authentic life and feel joy as I move about with passion and purpose. I need to liquidate some things to release the financial stress during this transition so tomorrow, I am going to sell my remaining jewelry on eBay, and I am going to stop looking for event and marketing jobs. Please align with me to make

this happen, and I want to be extremely specific that it needs

to happen quickly. I promise I will not confuse you with distorted energy any longer, as I know who I am, and I know what to pursue. You have always known my secret, and now my secret is shared between us to lighten my burden and pursue my greatest potential. I ask you with the utmost humility as I don't have a lot of time to squander, so we need to work together to make this happen expediently. I know I have said this twice now, as I feel my anxiety escalate and the fear creeping in through the cracks and crevices of my weakness and vulnerability. Please help me find alignment as an artist, as this is my true self, my authentic being, and I am exhausted trying to be someone else. I come to you, raw, vulnerable, and with the utmost humility as I search for a new path to call my own."

I began to sob and slowly picked myself up off the floor. I was dazed and a bit scared for my future, but I spoke with conviction, and felt I would rather die with nothing than live a lie and pursue someone else's life.

I could no longer be the old Greg, and there was no time to cocoon and hide inside a chrysalis to transition into my new form. Luckily the new form was already taking shape, simply by admitting the truth - so I guess it was always there but hidden away behind a mask that I believed was my authentic self. I took off my mask and was vulnerable to the world, and it felt exhilaratingly scary.

The following morning, I listed all my remaining jewelry on eBay in their illustrious auction format, and I looked only for artist jobs or creative jobs that would require my painting skill. As I was searching, I ran across a strange-looking ad on Craigslist. The ad was titled Paint & Sip, and the letters were in a variety of colors with a creative tagline that was suggestive and edgy.

The ad was looking for licensees to run their own business in Seattle while representing the brand and the brand guidelines. I liked the word licensee, as I was familiar with that term in the past, so I immediately felt some alignment, and I thought it would be interesting to run my own venture. The ad was simple at best and touted free beer and drink tickets upon arrival, which seemed a bit sketchy to me and sounded more like a ploy to get applicants to attend than a real job opportunity.

Initially I didn't want to respond to the ad, but this little voice in my head kept saying, "Just walk through the door, and if you don't like it, you can exit, but if you do nothing, then nothing happens." I decided to heed my own advice, and I applied. A few days later I was contacted by the organization, and they thanked me for applying, but they were looking for an artist who could create landscape paintings, and they considered me more of a portrait artist. I explained that portraits were much more difficult to create and whipped up a few landscape paintings for them to view on the fly. They enjoyed the submissions and asked me to attend the initial meeting at a local pub in Pioneer Square in Seattle, and they mentioned the drink tickets again, and I smirked with apprehension.

The weekend was fast approaching, and Saturday was the big day I would get my first free beer while attending a job interview. Drinking at a job interview tickled me a bit as I imagined a group of Seattleites sipping on home brews while listening to a corporate presentation on how one paints and drinks at the same time hoping to garner a solid result.

Saturday arrived, and I took an Uber downtown since parking was always a nightmare in that part of Seattle. I was the first to sign in, which was my usual protocol. I didn't like to stress out during the interview process, and I arrived pseudo early to prepare my mind for the initial greeting and questions that would be chaotically thrown at me as I would boomerang them back with some sense of articulateness.

A gentleman greeted me and handed me a drink ticket. He was in casual business attire, much like mine, and we connected immediately, as no one showed up for about thirty minutes, so we engaged in polite conversation. He stated he had a presentation to give, and he would dive into more detail and answer questions after the initial introduction to the brand. Thirty minutes later the room was filled with roughly fifteen people, and we all sat down as he began his spiel and we sipped on our free alcoholic beverage of choice.

This company was about drinking creatively, but what did it mean, and how did it blend the two together? A Master Artist walks you through a painting for two hours while you eat and drink with friends at a selected venue, and you take home your masterpiece. This sounded like a cool concept and certainly a unique event type. Another keyword that enticed me was the word "events."

As licensees, we would be producing paint and sip events that guests would enjoy throughout the Seattle area, and we would retain seventy percent of the total ticket price. The other thirty percent would go back to the corporate brand. Guests would purchase tickets on their website for forty-five dollars, so I whipped out my phone and started doing the math via the two percentages.

Most events held forty people, so forty times forty-five, minus thirty percent was a huge sum of money. Furthermore, I would be responsible for buying my own supplies, obtaining a business license, liability insurance, and hiring if I decided to go in that direction. I was super excited about the prospects of this venture as it utilized my favorite parts of my skillset: event planning, painting, and business management.

The presenter wrapped up the presentation stating that he was only taking one or two licensees for the entire area, and the rest would be declined the opportunity to move forward. I made eye contact with the corporate rep before departing, and he asked me what I thought about the venture and if it sounded like a lucrative opportunity. I explained that I was anxious and excited to build something I was passionate about and felt it was nice fit based on my past experience and my current love for the arts.

I loved the ripple effect of providing other artists the opportunity to paint and live an affordable lifestyle. This concept resonated with me and I felt a strong alignment upon arriving home and leisurely checked my email to see if any other artistic ventures landed in my inbox; to my surprise there was a contract waiting for me to move forward as the first paint and sip licensee in the Seattle area. This venture was swiftly happening, and God had provided an endless opportunity within a dynamic work setting in which I was perfectly matched. I barely read the fine print, signed the contract, and never looked back.

I would soon learn that the industry was vast, as there were mom and pop shops that were engaged in the paint and sip concept all around the city, but it was apparent there was still room for a premier brand. After signing the contract, Paul, the man who ran the presentation, gave me a call and wanted to get together on Sunday to venue hunt and secure some spaces for future events. I agreed, and we met in Ballard to discuss some of the backend tools on the admin panel portion of the website and he explained that they would allow me to load up venues, artist, paintings, and events. The location in Ballard was beautifully designed and sported a large private room in the back, which was more than suitable for large scale events.

We met with the GM who happened to be on site on a Sunday, which is more than rare in the restaurant industry, and he literally greenlit our events within five minutes of detailing the concept, and we agreed to move forward with Sundays at 2:00 p.m. My first venue was secured, and it was mindboggling to conceive that I was unemployed the day prior, and on Sunday I was a licensee for an upcoming premier brand that was quickly launching nationwide.

My soul was in a state of ecstasy, much like a tincture or potion when swallowed quickly provided an immediate burst of adrenalin and euphoria. I was surprised how quickly man-ifesting a desire could procreate into reality. It is our own limitation and thought process that speeds or slows the desires from colliding into our life, and it is the simple act of believing that speeds up the process so the arrival of our desires can expediently happen. It's important that ego is not in our way to ruin and obstruct the ultimate outcome. Being in a state of humility is in a sense being closer to divinity, and I firmly believe that the possibilities become greater when we are in our most humble state.

Tony Hsieh, the author of *Delivering Happiness* created a list of core values for his billion-dollar company, and humility always made the top ten list of his core values. Hitting rock bottom, simmering in the darkness, or hanging out in the abyss can reveal a greater sense of truth as the ego is torn apart and separated from the spirit. It is in this moment of clarity that we can swiftly move forward with conviction and a determination that is powerful and unstoppable. I don't wish anyone to suffer or hit their darkest moment in order to ascend to their greatest potential, but sometimes being uncomfortable and uncertain can reveal the ultimate truth. Humility creates an open portal and the answers become more fluid as the ego is separated and dissolved. Living in a state of gratitude and being grateful is another way of minimizing the ego and keeping it in check.

Paul discussed more details about the portal as he loaded up my first venue while constructing my artist profile and bio. We began the discussion about supplies and the financial aspect of the licensee contract, and Paul explained that corporate would purchase all of the supplies for the initial kit and deduct a small portion each week from my direct deposit until the kit was paid in full. What a great business model to help fund artists with little to no cash flow so they can help build an empire of creativity.

It was a brilliant concept, and I had no doubt that this venture was going to breed success as it felt joyful and invigorating. Hunting for venues wasn't my strong suit, but it was paramount in order to create joy and inspiration, so I had to learn to be gregarious and fun while searching for that perfect place where we would inspire guests in the future. Paul left on Monday, and I was left strolling around town convincing venues that this paint and sip concept was a new, profitable way to generate income, as we would bring in forty guests each week, and the venue would profit from the forty guests eating and drinking. Some spaces had their challenges and were too small or dark, while others had parking or carpeting issues (hard surfaced floors worked the best as the paint could easily be wiped up after each event).

At the end of the week I had four venues on board and gravitated toward those where I felt a semblance of partnership and positive energy from the staff and management. I was ready to load up events, but I had no visuals to entice guests to purchase tickets. Since this paint and sip brand was new, there was no painting library, so once I wrapped up the venue search, I painted three to five paintings a day and loaded them up in the library. A few weeks later I had over fifty paintings loaded in the admin portal and was well on my way to bringing in customers for future events.

The admin portal held a ton of information, as well as ticketing info and a variety of reports that we could run to check how our business was doing. I started monitoring ticket sales, and the events were magically filling up thanks to Groupon and their ability to secure new acquisitions quickly.

As I began running reports and diving into ticket totals, I was blindsided by the business model as a whole.

I didn't see any forty-five dollar tickets, but a slew of twenty-five dollar tickets instead. When I confronted Paul about the discrepancy, he explained that Headquarters (HQ) had to pay a large fee for Groupon, and that the Groupon ticket total would be twenty-five dollars not forty-five minus the thirty percent which Headquarters would take based on the signed contract. At that moment, I realized I had started building this mini empire, but the financials were going to be vastly different then on presentation day. I continued to do the math, and after buying supplies, it was still a nice sum of money even though it was half of what was initially presented. Paul explained that Groupon was used at the beginning as a new acquisition tool, and eventually people would buy full price tickets on their own.

My curiosity was satiated momentarily, and I focused on growing the business and expanding the painting library. My only regret was wishing there was more transparency up front as I'm sure Paul knew about Groupon and the payout prior to my signing. Startups did come with their own set of idiosyncrasies, and one needed to have an entrepreneurial spirit, so I slipped one on and flowed through the process.

The launch day arrived as I loaded up my car with canvas, paint, easels, table covers, paper towels, brushes, and more, and started setting up at the venue a couple hours prior to start time. My car wreaked of glue as the fresh canvas permeated the inside of my vehicle, and despite the chill in the air, my windows were left half open to abate the chemical odor and allow the fresh Seattle air to revitalize my lungs.

After arriving at the venue, my anxiety escalated a bit as I was extremely nervous and unsure about my unknown charismatic speaking abilities, but I knew I could paint, and if all else failed, the painting part was going to be exhilaratingly successful. This paint and sip brand had no onboarding process or even a video in which to view a full event. HQ gave me a little background and a brief script to follow, but it sounded too contrived, and not appropriate for the Seattle vibe.

I knew I was going to have to construct something different but wasn't quite certain as I had never walked anyone through a painting in two hours while they become buzzed on their libation of choice. Guests started to trickle in close to start time, but many weren't on my manifest. I would soon learn that if they bought a Groupon, that they needed to go to the website, select an event, enter the code, and redeem their voucher for a ticket.

This happened several times throughout the check-in process, and I instructed guests to go online and redeem their vouchers. Thankfully I had space for a few more guests, and things were going smoothly. The entire room was pre-set with an easel, canvas, paper towels, cup with water, and a plate with the primary colors of paint: blue, black, white, yellow, and red. Each guest would arrive, grab an apron, and take a seat. I decided if a guest left their seat, or wanted to save one for another guest, they should leave their apron wrapped around the back of the chair, and this system worked out well. Guests could arrive later and still have a reserved seat next to their friend. Check-in required thinking spontaneously while developing protocol and the best standards for the future.

Most guests arrived fifteen minutes prior to the start time, and I was bombarded as well as the bartender with drink orders and check-in details. I would find out later that HQ sent out event details to guests instructing them to arrive fifteen minutes prior to their event start time. I knew I couldn't have forty guests arriving at the same time for future events, so I had some work to do to curtail this event flow, but for now it was a bit messy. In the future I would figure out that I could contact guests prior to their event and explain seating, parking, and other pertinent information so they could have a more enjoyable paint and sip experience and arrive early to acclimate to their new environment while taking photos of the painting they were about to create.

It was ten minutes after the start time, and there were still four guests missing according to my manifest, but it was time to kick off my first event. I flicked on my lavalier microphone and headed toward the front of the room and introduced myself. I could tell the audience could feel my nervousness and apprehension. I simply needed to get through the introduction as quickly as possible to remove the spotlight from myself and have it focused on painting and the guests' empty canvases.

I explained that the red cups are not for drinking as they hold the paint water and rinsing of our brushes even though they look like beer cups from our college days, and I got a few laughs. Mixing of colors was a feature topic, and I moved quickly into the first base color of paint. "Okay everyone, we are now going to paint all of our canvases blue, and if you use a little white, they will become baby blue. I will paint this quickly so you can see the result, but please take your time and enjoy as I stroll through the room." To my amazement, the focus shifted from me to the canvas, and everyone in the room was talking, painting, and having fun.

I felt a huge sense of relief as the anxiety left my body, and I could focus on my happy place, which was painting. Everyone was cheerfully focused, and the canvases progressed as I presented the next step. Occasionally I would hold up a guest's canvas to inspire others to take a different journey and that following my master painting wasn't the focal point of the event. Two hours flew by, and I wrapped up the session explaining that I would take Facebook photos and post them later when I returned home. Guests came up to have their pictures taken with their finished canvases, and they smiled and thanked me for such a great night. I packed up my equipment, wiped up the floor, grabbed my tip jar, and returned to my car. I sat in my car for a moment reflecting on the evening, as I wasn't ready to drive off just yet. I was alive, overwhelmed, and excited that my little venture that I had been planning for eight weeks took flight, and I finished my first paint and sip Seattle Event with an extra added bonus of having cash in my pocket from my illustrious tip jar.

Producing events for the public and building a business meant that I needed to show up even during times of extreme stress. If I didn't work, I didn't get paid, and my guests would receive an urgent last-minute cancellation notice that would ruin their plans, birthday party, or other special moment they planned during their paint and sip event. These events were largely celebratory, and some individuals used this platform to propose to their special someone as they dropped to one knee and wrote will you marry me on their canvas. This business was a marriage, and I needed to show up through sickness and health until death do us part. There was no backup plan, and I was about to find out exactly what that meant, being the sole proprietor and sole performer of my own business.

I was loading into a venue on First Avenue, and it was crowded, noisy, and traffic was a beast. I illegally parked and dropped off my supplies, hop-ped back in my car, and headed toward a parking garage that closed shortly after my event ended. If I didn't make it out in time, my car would be closed inside the garage until the next morning. It wasn't the best option, but it was the closest garage I could find downtown that was somewhat adjacent to the venue, so I parked the car and walked back to the restaurant and began setting up in the backroom. I received a call on my cell phone, but the number was unrecognizable, so I let it go to voicemail and continued setting up. Halfway through setup I decided to check my voicemail as curiosity got the best of me, and it was the voice of my stepfather, who I hadn't heard from in decades, letting me know that my mother was passing away and only had a few hours left. In the voicemail he stated that it was difficult to find me and was hoping that this was the correct phone number and to call him back as soon as possible.

Why he gave me a few hours to say goodbye to my mother I will never understand, nor will I carry the burden of feeling angry toward him, so the only emotion I could muster was forgiveness. I felt a deep sadness and almost pathetic stance toward him, that he didn't provide me with more time to say goodbye to someone special, nor did he give me time to mend our brokenness and provide some semblance of healing and closure.

I had thirty-six guests coming to my event, and some had already trickled in. At this point I knew I couldn't cancel, so I ran to the stairwell, undulating inside from an emotional overload, tears strewn down my face. I'm not sure where I found the strength to persevere, but the guests arrived, and I put on a show and gave a performance worthy of an Oscar, or at least I thought so as I was in an incredible amount of pain distraught from the news, and I masked it as best I could. Occasionally I would turn to my canvas and pretend I was painting and wipe away some tears with a paper towel that I happened to have in my pocket at the time. I finished the event and even sang happy birthday to a group of girls that were celebrating. The moment the last guest left, I curled up into a ball, and began shuddering on the hardwood floor.

One of the guests happened to leave her coat behind, and she walked back into the room and found me curled in a ball much like a beetle that had just been poked by some wooden stick or nipped by a predator. She asked me if things were okay, and with a barely audible voice I explained that my mom was dying, and she came over and gave me a tender hug and shook her head in disbelief that I produced an entire event with this looming over my head. I simply explained that this was my business, and the show must go on. I tried to crack a small smile as the blurred vision of the onlooker became more and more difficult to see, tears providing an impressionist back drop of misty colors and undefined lines.

Later that evening I said my final goodbye to Mom over the phone. It certainly wasn't optimal, but I wasn't given an optimized choice, so I took it and embraced it. Shortly after our call she passed away, and I would find out later that her last words she whispered were "my baby, my baby" as she closed her eyes and took her last breath. She thought of me, and I was her final imprint before she said goodbye as she left the planet and her earthly possessions behind to embark on her new journey. I needed this closure, and it helped to slowly suture my fragmented heart and heavy spirit as I tried to move on and close the chapter of the book titled *My Broken Childhood*.

It is sometimes during the darkest hour that we somehow find the brightest light that guides us forward and fills us with a simple surge of strength and conviction. I slowly poured my soul into my small business and watched it spring forth with abundance.

At this point I was the only artist, and if I didn't show up, the event didn't happen, so I ate healthy and took care of my body and was steadfast in my belief that this business model would work. I told myself to believe that I was on the right track and believe that I was placed here for a reason and to feel the love in the room and focus on the alignment of this new venture. There was genuine love in the room each time I performed, and I did my best to swallow as much as I could to replenish my energy and fuel myself up for the following day.

Months passed and the events became richer oozing with spiritual nuggets as I became more comfortable with my audience and myself. My intro incorporated humor, and I spoke about the events being a judgement-free zone where we could all paint with the support and love from others. Whatever happened outside of these doors was not important, because these events were a safe place to express ourselves without being critiqued. The guests loved the freedom and flexibility of the events, and my spiritual awareness and intuition grew as I connected deeply with the customers through solid eye contact or reading their paintings and brushstrokes. It was easy to see who needed a bit more love and attention in the room, while others were fine painting and enjoying the quality time away from their smartphone. Each guest had an expectation, and it was up to me to understand that expectation and to fulfill it by connecting and touching each one through conversation, interaction, and providing positive energy.

Often, I would begin my introduction, and someone in the room would be giving me some incredible eye contact or smiling so big that their energy filled the space. I would stop right in the middle of my intro and walk over to that person and ask their name. They would reply, and I would talk about their energy, and how they walked in with zero anxiety, and I would give them my card and offer them a free ticket to a future event. This would also allow me to segue into a discussion about anxiety and what it meant and how it handcuffed us from being our best self. The event sessions became little mini-therapy sessions as I touched on our disconnectedness during the Digital Age and spoke about how we can reconnect through our creative experience. This concept of therapy and art became so popular that my events started selling out, and it was time to expand.

I needed to hire, and I needed to do it quickly, but I was so fearful of managing another artist who would be a front facing asset of the business. I had grown the business to a meaningful stage, and it would be critical to find the right people to help me grow it further. I was apprehensive about my first hire, so I decided to incorporate some healing aspect in my ad to attract someone more intuitive. It was important to find someone who loved to connect with people on a deeper level and provide a little healing at an event as well as walking guests through a painting. I posted my first ad on Craigslist and received a slew of applications.

Most of the applicants didn't follow instructions well, and they wouldn't attach their artwork or lead me to their website where I could review their work. Some had a ton of typos in their cover letter, and some had no cover letter at all. It was up to me to sift through the multitude of weeds and find the four-leaf clover. I decided to tier the interview process into three parts. The first part was a brief phone interview that lasted about fifteen minutes. I could hear tonal quality, how quickly they articulated, and if they cared about their life and had passion for the arts. The second phase was an in-person interview where I could assess eye contact, anxiety levels, and confidence.

The last part of the interview required attending one of my events and watching me in action absorbing the event flow and interaction with each guest. Each candidate was told to arrive two hours early to see my setup, and some would volunteer to assist while others would get a drink at the bar and watch. At the end of the event, I would ask the remaining candidates what they thought and listened to their feedback. It was important to listen more and talk less as they explained their theory about the event and how they would have done it differently. One artist brought his portfolio with him, and it really set him apart from the other candidates.

He seemed quieter and not as outgoing as the others, but I felt that he would be easier to mold and manage. He had a kindness in his eyes that was sincere, and I knew he would care about the guests and the guests' experience. I conducted a brief background check, made an offer and hired my first paint and sip Seattle Artist.

After hiring, I required additional onboarding at my apartment where I explained the admin portal, and the tips and tricks of walking a large group through a challenging painting. I had a traditional contract and noncompete, which needed to be signed, and I took a photo of his driver's license, and his signed W-9. I explained the paid painting program and that he was allowed to paint originals for the platform, and if anyone used them across the U.S. and Canada, he would receive royalties of ten dollars for each use. He was excited about the idea of making additional income painting, and he shook my hand, smiled, and a few weeks later ran his first event.

As the business expanded, I would find myself going through this same process five more times, until I had a team of six artists, and was running one hundred and twenty events per month. Business was booming, and the concept was fresh as events filled up from Seattle all the way to Olympia. As with many ventures in life, there were many more tests that would come my way, and I would need to grow a tremendous amount if I were going to survive them. I couldn't imagine or design the hurdles that I would jump through to keep this business alive and it was probably one of the biggest adventures of my lifetime.

HQ started accumulating quite a few licensees on the platform, so they created a page where we could all share ideas and discuss the business. They expanded rapidly as we did and soon had over one-hundred and fifty licensees running the same business in almost every city nationwide.

This paint and sip company became a recognizable brand and won several awards out of the gate and was touted as a fifty-five million dollar company almost overnight. With such quick success, HQ decided to throw an event called the Paint and Sip Palooza, and they would invite all the licensees across the nation to gather in one place to share ideas and brainstorm. Licensees had an opportunity to present, and there were breakout sessions, which included more detail about hiring, how to launch successful social media campaigns, and inventory management and kit sharing. The Palooza was to be held in Las Vegas, and there were about eighty licensees in attendance.

Most of them, like myself, had started their business in 2013. HQ management would present during the main session, and then the breakout sessions would occur later on that day, run by seasoned licensees. It's important to note that as this corporation expanded, so did their team of new hires at HQ, and soon there were several C-suite employees, as well as VPs, and Directors. Every division had a VP, and at this point they were broken down into these departments: Customer Service, Private Events, Finance, Marketing, Tech, Licensee Relations, Recruiting and General Operations. The new hires had some savvy tech background, but few, if any, had any creative or artistic background. It would be interesting to see a visually creative company being run by tech savvy individuals with no visual arts training. The two co-owners were still involved at this point of the venture, so there would still be some symmetry between the corporate new hires and the soul of the company.

It was Palooza's first main session, and we were all wide eyed with our laptops open, eager to savor each morsel that sped our way. The Chief Operating Officer stood in the front of the room and began a presentation about their overall success, and we were all excited to share in her enthusiasm. As the presentation progressed, she casually mentioned that HQ would begin taking "Marketing Commissions," and we would see three dollars or more being taken from each ticket depending on how the guest purchased their ticket. She mentioned some additional fees that would be tacked onto our reports, including credit cards fees, and she quickly moved on to another subject. Her voice was shrill, and the pitch was awkwardly disturbing, so many of us were happy to see her finish her presentation and segue with another presenter.

Most, if not all, were still digesting the past presentation, and we couldn't quite wrap our heads around what just transpired. Sadly, the rest of the presentations had little to no impact as we were still simmering about these additional fees and what it would mean to our business, the business that we had built from the ground up. The energy in the room shifted much like a skylight veiled underneath a blackened cloud, and despair and confusion slowly filled the room. The additional fees were the core topic at cocktail parties and dinners throughout the Palooza, and we all left after three days of presentations feeling sullen and lifeless.

Months would follow, and the original contract of a seventy/thirty split became an even fifty-fifty split as the additional fees shredded our profit and loss, and suddenly I didn't have enough set aside to pay my quarterly taxes. One of the owners ended up being paid out and left; it was the one who had originally recruited me. I respected him a great deal and could totally understand why he would want to leave an organization who had vastly strayed from its original vision.

He wanted to provide jobs for artists who would normally not have such an abundant financial outlet to pursue. It was a brilliant concept but was now interceded with a hidden agenda, and most of it was surrounded by taking the company public and prepping the selling portfolio to look tastier for investors. HQ received thirteen million dollars in funding during their first investor round and found themselves with a full Board of Directors, some of them being venture capitalists. The company may have been on their way to becoming an IPO, but at what price? We were distraught and uncertain about our future; a future that we built from zero, and yet it wasn't ours to own.

CHAPTER 6

HQ

Ego and Greed are destructive foes
Cunning and mischievous
Fearless and senseless
Their synergy like the Angel of Death
As they scythe down the innocence
And devour their prey to bones and dust remain
My fog-filled mind blindly sees
I'm lost beneath the dew
Slowly sunken slinking sun
Will thou appear to sing

As licensees, we banded together, running reports and comparing data. Many consulted with attorneys showing them our initial contract and noncomplete clause that inhibited us from working in any type of similar industry for one year after our departure from the corporation. Some of us started writing into HQ Support describing our financial scenarios, and how our business was no longer profitable. Some of the marketing fees exceeded seven dollars per ticket, and we simply couldn't survive with the crumbs we were handed after the fees were taken out of our direct deposits each week. Many had to reduce the salaries they were paying their artists, and we lost our teams and had to start over with new wages and new expectations in order to survive. It was a difficult time, and the ultimate test of perseverance and survival for all of us. We all wanted to make this business work, and none of us wanted to give it up, but slowly key individuals departed from the platform.

I remember the day when Brian left the platform, and the note he left for all of us to ponder. Brian was the first licensee to join this corporation, and he was the best performer nationwide. He grew an incredible business, and after years of being the spokesperson for the company, he decided to pursue his original business as a welder and DJ.

He left all of us a note, and we listened intently as he explained that his passion withered much like a grape that spent too many hours in the sun and was bled dry by its blistering rays, transforming itself into another form all together. Many believe a raisin is more powerful than a grape as it has harnessed its transformation from the sun, but Brian didn't feel powerful. His sadness and disappointment left an indelible scar, one that he feared would never depart, as he said his goodbyes and left the platform for good.

HQ sent out messages to the licensees explaining that we shouldn't panic or worry, that this was normal for a startup, and there would be bumps in the road. Their correspondence became convoluted with automation and technology, machine-like contrived responses that lacked a sense of caring and personality. I loved the business, but my passion too was slowly diminishing as I felt my alignment slip away and yearned for 2013 again when I felt soulful and alive.

HQ began placing multiple licensees in the larger markets, so a competitive war began in the larger cities, including Seattle. It was a battle each day as I would awaken, slip on my armor and choose my weapon of choice as a means of survival. Each licensee had permission to venture into another's venue and produce events on another night or across the street as there were no dividing lines, and chaos ensued.

I remember creating a hashtag for my team and inserting this hashtag at the end of the artist's last name so that guests could align themselves with my team, as it worked as a branding tool and set our team apart from the others. Our events were more spiritual and healing in nature, and guests aligned with our mission and core values. Love was our message, and the support and kindness we gave was the added value guests were starving for, and we continued to pour our soul into each event. Slowly guests started buying tickets around the other licensee and chose to come to our team events and not the other. It was vicious and ugly, as the other licensee's tactic was to secure as many venues as he could so that I couldn't expand my business further, and I wouldn't have any venues in which to produce any future events. I would learn patience, and that joy and harmony were not based on conditions but were choices that I made daily. My team was extremely supportive, and after two years of branding with my hashtag, the other licensee slowly faded in the distance and was gone. I never wished ill of him and always felt that if his tactics stemmed from a kinder place, he certainly would have survived. Vicious intentions breed instability and chaos. Without love and passion for others, our selfish desires and ego ultimately consume us.

HQ changed regimes several times, trying to revitalize the essence of 2013, and promising a better future full of theories and concepts that were not previously tried. The focus on the future, and the lack of being present provided obstacles that were insurmountable as the soul of the company diminished and the tech savvy future stepped in to try and save the day. Living in the future is difficult. You can't listen to the voices in the present, because you aren't here to digest them. You make decisions that you believe are concrete, but you don't have the present voices to give you balance and provide you with input and viable feedback. It's a dangerous place to live, and certainly not sustainable.

I am happy to say that a final regime did step in, one that floundered a bit, and at times lost their way as the Board shifted, and key executives were reassigned or fired. As licensees we spoke our mind and created a council that met with the Vice President on a weekly basis. She was kind, compassionate, and empathetic to our cause. She sent out surveys and gathered information about our business backgrounds while assessing the current pulse and life of the company. She reviewed licensee's profits and losses, those that were willing to trust her, and she began piecing the convoluted puzzle together.

It was enlightening to say the least, and at the last hour of the last day, after several key licensees departed from the platform, HQ vowed to abolish all marketing commissions and began rebuilding their relationship with those that helped to build theirs. It was a monumental victory, one that felt very God-like, as there was little hope that a corporation could move from being greedy and egocentric to evolving into a corporation that cared for the business and wanted to align with the partners that helped it initially succeed.

I am still on this journey. I find great joy in many of its gifts, and I remind myself of those gifts daily. Sifting in a mindset of gratitude heals brokenness and shifts our focus on what we are grateful for, rather than focusing on what is missing. Being a small-business owner provides jobs for artists in my area and gives venues additional income they would normally miss.

We provide inspiration and healing for others and an outlet to express yourself creatively without judgment or critique. We provide joy, and it is this joy that continues to fill my heart and allows me to move forward with conviction, and as long as I retain this joy, I will continue this journey. The ripple effect of providing love and inspiration for others is never ending, and I feel its pulse daily as I am reminded through email, texts, and event photos that illuminate my heart and mind.

I am finally on the right path, and although there were tenuous moments and times of doubt, I did believe this would work. It is this simple, positive thought of believing that ultimately made it possible to persevere through the sadness and disappointment of the business. The joy outlived the sadness. The love outlived the disappointment. The business was a resolute one, which made it that much easier to believe. We all hold this power inside of us, the power and will to manifest our desires with unwavering conviction and watch them all unfold before us by simply believing.

CHAPTER 7

Epilogue

Believe in you, I do
Take all that blind incongruity
And toss it aside as you would an empty tin of
unwantedness
Keep within you the strength to believe
And with this simple gift, you shall capture the
world

Keeping the strength to believe is a war that rages inside most of us, as we fight within ourselves to surrender to that belief with ultimate conviction. Once we surrender and reside in that humble place, our alignment shifts and allows the gifts to come forth in abundance. As I traverse back to my childhood days, many might have voted me most likely to end my life during uncertain times of chaos and depression. I might have agreed with them, but there was also something inside of me that was driving me forward, and there's something inside all of us. An invisible force that propels us to a place where we believe we can be better, happier, more fulfilled, more loving, and kinder. Some simply call it God. Many people ask me about my religion, and I tell them, "Love is my religion." I strive to be the most loving individual I can be during the challenges and obstacles that are thrown my way on Planet Earth.

I try to mitigate the mind-chatter in order to stay present and engage in acts of kindness, while listening to other people's pain and hardship. I live by this quote by Ralph Waldo Emerson: "Knowing that one life has breathed easier because you have lived, this is to have succeeded." This is my *religion*. I don't go to church on Sundays, but I make church a daily routine.

I walk the line of love as much as possible. This is my *church*, and when we decide to live it, life gets better. When we decide to believe, it's a powerful gift. The greatest gift we can give ourselves is the power to believe, the power to believe we can do things without fear and without worrying about this fictitious word called "failure."

Many live a conditional life, and it is these conditions that form their thoughts and feelings. God gave us freewill so that we could choose our feelings and state of mind without relying on these conditions to dictate our mindset. Some can be stricken with a terminal illness and be more joyful than an individual who appears to have it all. Joy is a choice. Happiness is a choice. Love is a choice and being a loving being is a choice.

I didn't always understand myself, but I searched for the meaning and hidden purpose as joy and happiness would slowly come forward to greet me. I experienced great sadness too with the passing of my parents and the chaos that ensued. My awareness of mortality blossomed as action became more poignant and sitting around listening to my inner chatter became less relevant. My mind and ego were in the way most of the time, but the world has a way of pummeling us through life's lessons and sanding us down to reveal the diamond beneath. It is at this moment that our humility surfaces to provide a greater understanding of ourselves, our surroundings, and our sense of purpose.

I always know when I am in my most humble state, because this is also when I am most approachable as babies, dogs, and people of all walks of life seem to be magnetically drawn to my presence. It's almost incomprehensible how our energy resonates and bounces off others as it permeates through our environment and creates a joyful ripple effect when we let it.

On the other hand, my moments that lack humility tend to breed hostility and anger as I venture through my environment closed off, unapproachable, and usually ignored by others. Negative thoughts create clutter and mind chatter as I bounce from past to future, unable to remain and absorb or enjoy my present moment. Being in a state of humility is paramount, as well as being present. If we are not present, then where are we and how can we make an impact if we're not even here?

Most importantly, don't take life too seriously. While you're here, be here, be present, and move forward as the fearless warrior you were meant to be. Don't listen to the dream killers. There are more of them than of us, and they would do anything to remove that little fire you have burning that infuses you to create something unique and special. Surround yourself with good people who believe in you and love you. Minimize the toxicity and emphasize the joy. Do acts of kindness daily whether you open a door for someone or simply say good morning to a stranger. Open yourself up to new experiences and always remember one important thing:

"We are not human beings having a spiritual experience. We are spiritual beings having a human experience." – *Father Pierre Teilhard de Chardin.*

Love and Light.
GC

ABOUT THE AUTHOR

GREGORY COPPLOE is a Poet, Author, Professional Artist, and Life Coach. He is a four-time American Art Award Winner, and a graduate of UCLA in Theatre Arts. Mr. Copploe's work in Hollywood spanned two decades and was the catalyst for his search for his true self and greater purpose as he left toxicity behind. Mr. Copploe is an avid believer in living in the present moment, releasing fear, and nurturing meaningful connections that trigger joyful experiences. Gregory may be reached through his website: www.gregorycopploe.com.

ABOUT
KHARIS PUBLISHING

KHARIS PUBLISHING is an independent, traditional publishing house with a core mission to publish impactful books, and channel proceeds into establishing mini-libraries or resource centers for orphanages in developing countries, so these kids will learn to read, dream, and grow. Every time you purchase a book from Kharis Publishing or partner as an author, you are helping give these kids an amazing opportunity to read, dream, and grow. Kharis Publishing is an imprint of Kharis Media LLC. Learn more at https://www.kharispublishing.com.

THE ART OF BEING WHOLE

CPSIA information can be obtained
at www.ICGtesting.com
Printed in the USA
FSHW020106300919
62506FS